3-MINUTE
PRAYERS
for the Worried Heart

© 2022 by Barbour Publishing, Inc.

Print ISBN 978-1-63609-415-1

Published by Barbour Publishing, Inc., 1810 Barbour Drive, Uhrichsville, Ohio 44683, www.barbourbooks.com

Our mission is to inspire the world with the life-changing message of the Bible.

Printed in China.

Renae Brumbaugh Green

3-MINUTE PRAYERS

for the Worried Heart

Comfort and Peace for Women

BARBOUR
PUBLISHING

Introduction

Quiet down before GOD, be prayerful before him.
PSALM 37:7 MSG

These encouraging prayers are especially for those days when you are weary from the busyness of everyday life, when the cares of this world weigh you down, when your soul longs for quiet refreshment in the Creator's presence. Three minutes from your hectic day is all you'll need to fill your cup to overflowing with strength for life's journey.

- Minute 1: Read and reflect on God's Word.
- Minute 2: Pray, using the provided prayer to jump-start a conversation with God.
- Minute 3: Reflect on a question for further thought.

Although this book isn't meant as a tool for deep Bible study, each soul-stirring prayer can be a touchstone to keep you grounded and focused on the One who hears all your prayers. May this book remind you that the heavenly Father cares about everything you face. Go on. . .talk to Him today. He's ready and waiting to hear from you!

Casting Practice

> *Cast your cares on the LORD and he will sustain you; he will never let the righteous be shaken.*
> PSALM 55:22 NIV

Dear Father,

It's interesting that You tell us to cast our cares on You. Casting something requires effort on my part. The greater the effort, the stronger the cast will be. The more I practice, the better my aim. You want to see that I'm willing to grab all my cares, all my worries and anxieties, put some muscle behind them, and throw them Your way. When I'm worried about something, I tend to freeze up. I stand there, holding my problems, hoping You'll come and take them from me. No more, Father. Today, I cast it all on You. Each time a worrisome thought enters my mind, I'll throw it with all my might in Your direction, for I know You care about every detail of my life.

What things will you cast on the Father today?

God of Details

*In the beginning, God created the heavens
and the earth. The earth was without form
and void, and darkness was over the face
of the deep. And the Spirit of God was
hovering over the face of the waters.*
GENESIS 1:1-2 ESV

Dear Father,

I've read this scripture many times, but it's comforting to come back to this starting point. Before time began, You were there. Why do I worry about my problems when I know the infinite God of the universe is in control? You created every good thing. Without You, nothing would exist. You placed the sun in the sky, scattered the stars like glitter, and positioned the moon just so. You saw to every facet of creation, and You still oversee it all today. I know You can—and will—take care of every detail of my life.

What details will you entrust to the Creator today?

Generous Father

*And God said, "Let the earth sprout vegetation,
plants yielding seed, and fruit trees bearing
fruit in which is their seed, each according
to its kind, on the earth." And it was so.*

GENESIS 1:11 ESV

Dear Father,

You are so generous with us! When I think of fruits and vegetables I grow in my garden or buy at the store, I realize within that single fruit is the potential for dozens, even hundreds more plants. Each seed can produce countless more of its kind, and each of those can produce countless more, and on and on. Your design provides perfectly for all our needs. Why do I worry about what my family will eat, what we'll wear, or how I'll pay the bills? I trust You to provide everything I need. Your generosity overwhelms me.

What kinds of things do you need God to provide for you?

God's Smile

*So God created the great sea creatures and every
living creature that moves, with which the waters
swarm, according to their kinds, and every winged bird
according to its kind. And God saw that it was good.*
GENESIS 1:21 ESV

Dear Father,

You must have had so much fun creating all the sea creatures! I can just imagine You laughing, showing Jesus and the Holy Spirit, saying, "Look! This one has eight legs." Then You moved on to the birds, painting their feathers in the most glorious colors, positioning each one just so, to make flight possible. If You took that much time and detail with sea creatures and birds, You must have been even more excited to create me—a person in Your image. When I doubt myself, when I feel anxious about my place in the world, remind me that You created each living thing for Your pleasure, and that includes me. May my words, thoughts, and actions bring You pleasure today, Lord.

How will you make God smile today?

In Your Image

So God created mankind in his own image,
in the image of God he created them;
male and female he created them.
GENESIS 1:27 NIV

Dear Father,

Thank You for this reminder that I was made in Your image. So often, I hear voices in my head that tell me I'm not good enough, not attractive enough, not smart enough, that I'll never measure up. The lies are loud, and they just keep coming. But according to Your Word, I'm made in the image of the perfect, holy, almighty, eternal God. When I doubt myself, remind me of who I am, Lord. Help me to become more and more like You as I develop traits of compassion, kindness, gentleness, and love. When those voices speak, help me silence them. After all, I am a daughter of the Most High God.

What traits do you have that resemble God's character?

Time for Rest

*Then God blessed the seventh day and
made it holy, because on it he rested from all
the work of creating that he had done.*
GENESIS 2:3 NIV

Dear Father,

Thank You for this reminder that You rested. I feel like
I'm running all the time, Lord. There's always something to
do, someone to take care of, some meal to cook or mess to
clean or responsibility to tend to. Even when I try to rest, my
mind races. I know I feel more anxious about things when
I'm tired. I know hard work pleases You, but frantic, nonstop
busyness doesn't. Do I even know how to relax, Lord? I want
to follow Your example of resting after my work. Will You
show me how? Today, help me remember to take time to just
rest in Your love, in Your joy, in Your peace.

What will you do differently today so you can rest in Him?

Deep Breath

*Then the LORD God formed a man from the dust of
the ground and breathed into his nostrils the breath
of life, and the man became a living being.*

GENESIS 2:7 NIV

Dear Father,

You took such special care in making us. You breathed Your own breath into us! Why do I ever doubt Your love for me? Whenever I feel anxious, remind me to breathe. With each breath I take, remind me that it's Your breath giving me life, filling my lungs, spreading to every part of me. Let me feel Your beautiful, serene peace as I relax in Your care. Each time I inhale, bring my thoughts to Your great love, and each time I exhale, help me picture all the worries and cares leaving my body, scattering in the wind. Thank You for Your breath that gives me life.

How will you remind yourself to take deep breaths today?

A Real Place

A river watering the garden flowed from Eden;
from there it was separated into four headwaters.
GENESIS 2:10 NIV

Dear Father,

It's hard to imagine that Eden was a real place. It's so far removed from my reality that, as much as I try, I can't picture it. But You created the garden perfectly. Before You created man and woman in Your image, You had everything ready for them so they'd lack for nothing. Sin destroyed Your perfect plan, but it didn't destroy Your love for us. When I feel worried, anxious, and stressed, bring to mind this beautiful place called Eden. Remind me that even now, You're preparing a place for me in heaven, and it will be more glorious than anything I can imagine. Thank You for Jesus and for Your abundant provision for my life both now and for eternity.

When you picture heaven, what do you see?

Making Friends

*The LORD God said, "It is not good for the man to
be alone. I will make a helper suitable for him."*

GENESIS 2:18 NIV

Dear Father,

You said in Your Word that it's not good for us to be
alone. Yet I often feel lonely, Father. Even though I know
there are people in my life who care about me, it's hard for
me to connect with them. Sometimes I worry about what
they'll think or if they're judging me. This fear forces a wall
around me and keeps me from deepening my friendships.
Whether it's with my spouse, my children, or others in my
life, help me to love without fear, Father. Help me focus on
others instead of myself. Send people I can connect with,
and help me develop the friendships I need to stay healthy
and accountable.

*What can you do today to connect with
others and deepen your friendships?*

Satan's Schemes

*Now the serpent was more crafty than any other
beast of the field that the LORD God had made.
He said to the woman, "Did God actually say,
'You shall not eat of any tree in the garden'?"*
GENESIS 3:1 ESV

Dear Father,

Satan hasn't changed his tactics at all. Just as he spoke to Eve in the garden and made her doubt herself and her convictions, he speaks to me in my head all the time. He causes me to doubt what I know is right. He makes me question Your love, Your power, Your faithfulness. When I question who You are and who I am in You, worry is born. Anxiety flourishes in this setting. When Satan plants seeds of doubt in my mind, help me recognize his craftiness and his lies. Make me strong in You. Make me confident in Your promises. Give me the assertiveness to put Satan in his place and call him a liar.

How has Satan caused you to doubt God?

Innocent

Then the LORD God said to the woman,
"What is this you have done?" The woman
said, "The serpent deceived me, and I ate."
GENESIS 3:13 NIV

Dear Father,

Before sin entered our lives, we were innocent. You perfectly provided for all our needs. After sin, our innocence was lost, and our lives became hard. Something inside me longs for that innocence, Lord. You created me in Your image, but sin has marred that image. You formed me, but sin has de-formed me. Before sin, we didn't have to worry about anything, did we? Fear wasn't in the human vocabulary. Help me remember, today and every day, that fear is not from You. Fear is from Satan, and it's not a part of Your plan for my life. Help me trust in You with the innocence of a child.

Can you recall a time of innocence in your life
when you didn't worry about anything?

When We Mess Up

The LORD God made garments of skin for
Adam and his wife and clothed them.
GENESIS 3:21 NIV

Dear Father,

This verse so perfectly illustrates who You are. Even though Adam and Eve disobeyed You, You still loved them. You still cared for them and provided for their needs. Instead of responding in anger, You gave them clothes to wear. So many times, I recognize my faults and my mistakes, and I worry that I'm not good enough. I worry that I'll be punished, rejected for my shortcomings. Father, even though others on this earth may judge me harshly, even though they may reject me, I know You never will. All Your actions toward me are born of love not anger. For that reason, I want to obey You. I want to serve You not out of fear but from a grateful heart.

In what way have you messed up and
worried you'd be rejected for it?

In His Presence

*Then Cain went away from the presence of the LORD
and settled in the land of Nod, east of Eden.*

GENESIS 4:16 ESV

Dear Father,

I don't ever want to leave Your presence. In Your presence, there is joy. There is peace. There is the quiet confidence that I'm wanted, I'm loved, and I belong. But outside Your presence, I find fear and anxiety and every bad thing. When I'm far from You, that's when worry takes over my mind. Forgive me for wandering away from You, Lord. Help me rest in You and delight in Your company. Next time I start to drift away, pull me back. Don't let me go, Father. Even when I'm stubborn and try to fight You, hold on to me. I want to live in Your presence every day, every hour, every minute of my life.

*Are you living in God's presence, or have
you wandered away from Him?*

I Need You

*At that time people began to call
upon the name of the LORD.*
GENESIS 4:26 ESV

Dear Father,

Why did it take people so long to recognize their need for You? If they had called on You sooner, they could have avoided so much heartache. Sin wouldn't have entered the world. Cain wouldn't have killed his brother, breaking his parents' hearts. So many hard things happened, all because they didn't call on You. The same thing is true in my life, Father. When I fail to recognize my need for You, bad things happen. When I don't call on You, life is harder than it needs to be. Help me learn the lesson early and never forget it. I need You. I will call on You every day. I find peace in knowing You will always hear me and You will always answer.

*Have you called upon God today
and shared your need with Him?*

Walk with God

*Enoch walked with God after he fathered Methuselah
300 years and had other sons and daughters. Thus
all the days of Enoch were 365 years. Enoch walked
with God, and he was not, for God took him.*

GENESIS 5:22–24 ESV

Dear Father,

What a testimony is contained in these three short verses! Enoch walked with *You*. He lived a long, faithful life, and You spared him from death and took him straight home. I want to live like that, Lord. I want to walk with You. I know from experience that when I stay close to You, when I think about Your promises and talk to You in my heart all day long, worry fades. When worry crowds in today, take my hand, Lord. Remind me of Your presence, and help me focus on You. I want each breath, each step to be in time with You.

*What do you think it means to
walk with God like Enoch did?*

Promise Keeper

*And God said, "This is the sign of the covenant
that I make between me and you and every living
creature that is with you, for all future generations:
I have set my bow in the cloud, and it shall be a sign
of the covenant between me and the earth."*

GENESIS 9:12-13 ESV

Dear Father,

Thank You for this reminder that You always keep Your promises. Every time I see a rainbow, I know You are faithful and true. The promise to never again destroy the earth by flood is just one of Your many promises to mankind and to me, personally. You've promised never to leave me or forsake me. You've promised to take care of me. You've promised to give me peace. The more time I spend in Your Word, the more promises I find. Your faithfulness in every area of my life serves as a gentle reminder that I don't need to worry about anything.

Which of God's promises do you need to remember today?

Abram's Example

*The Lord had said to Abram, "Go from your
country, your people and your father's household
to the land I will show you. I will make you into
a great nation, and I will bless you; I will make
your name great, and you will be a blessing."*

GENESIS 12:1–2 NIV

Dear Father,

Abram provides such a great example for me today. You told him to go, but You didn't tell him the destination. You just said, "I'll let you know when you get there." So Abram obeyed, without knowing the future. This is what faith looks like. When it comes to the future, I tend to worry and fret. I want to know what will happen and that it will go the way I want it to. Help me to have Abram's faith. Help me to trust You so much that I'll blindly say, "I don't know what will happen, but I know God will eventually bring me to a good place."

With what situation do you need to trust God today?

Back to the Beginning

From the Negev he went from place to place
until he came to Bethel, to the place between
Bethel and Ai where his tent had been earlier
and where he had first built an altar. There
Abram called on the name of the LORD.
GENESIS 13:3-4 NIV

Dear Father,

It's interesting that Abram went back to where You showed him in the beginning. Why did he leave there in the first place? Why do I walk away from the places and things You show me? Do I think the world can offer anything better than my loving heavenly Father? Forgive me for seeking security outside of Your love, outside of Your promises. Help me rest in Your goodness and stay in Your presence. When I feel anxious and worried, ground me, Father, and pull me back to my safe place—right in Your arms.

Do you need to return to God's presence
and rest in His promises today?

My Shield

*After these things the word of the LORD came to
Abram in a vision, saying, "Do not fear, Abram, I am
a shield to you; Your reward shall be very great."*

GENESIS 15:1 NASB

Dear Father,

When I read this verse, I know I can substitute my own name for Abram's. When I feel worried and afraid, I can hear You saying, "Do not fear, ___. I'm your shield." You truly are my Protector, Lord. I know You surround me, and You'll guard me from Satan's arrows. Even when bad things happen, I know You're right there with me, fighting for me. I don't have to do anything except trust You and stay close to You. When Satan tries to draw me away from Your presence by pulling me into worry and fear, remind me that he is a liar, and pull me back to You. Thank You for being my shield, Father.

*Against what circumstance do
you need God to be your shield?*

The Fixer

So Sarai said to Abram, "See now, the LORD
has prevented me from bearing children.
Please have relations with my slave woman;
perhaps I will obtain children through her."
And Abram listened to the voice of Sarai.

GENESIS 16:2 NASB

Dear Father,

Sarai tried to fix things. Instead of trusting You to keep Your promise to her, she took things into her own hands. How often do I do the same thing? I trust You for a little while, but when answers don't come and problems aren't solved as quickly as I hoped, I jump in and try to control the situation. I think I can fix things, instead of trusting You. Forgive me for that, Lord. Help me to be patient and trust Your timing instead of worrying and fretting and trying to manipulate things to go the way I think they should go.

What situation have you tried to fix recently?

Run to Him

When he raised his eyes and looked, behold, three men were standing opposite him; and when he saw them, he ran from the tent door to meet them and bowed down to the ground, and said, "My Lord, if now I have found favor in Your sight, please do not pass Your servant by."

GENESIS 18:2-3 NASB

Dear Father,

I love this picture of Abraham running to meet You. Scholars say these three men were Your Holy Trinity: Father, Son, and Holy Spirit. Abraham was so excited by Your presence that he ran to meet You. He begged You to stay with Him. Am I that excited to spend time with You, Lord? I want to be. I want to see You. I want to be in Your presence, for I know that's where I'll find the peace I long for. My request is the same: if I've found favor in Your sight, please don't pass me by.

Are you excited by God's presence?
Do you run to Him each day?

Thinking Too Small

So Sarah laughed to herself, saying, "After I have become old, am I to have pleasure, my lord being old also?"
GENESIS 18:12 NASB

Dear Father,

It's easy to judge Sarah for laughing, because I know the end of the story. I know that despite her age, she did have a son, and that was the beginning of the nation of Israel. But if I'd been in her place, I might have laughed too. How often do I think something is too big or too hard for You? How often do I look at a problem and think it's an impossible situation? Instead of trusting Your sovereignty, I worry and fret. Teach me to have Abraham's faith, Father. Help me to believe Your promises for yesterday, today, and all future days. Forgive me for thinking too small for You, Lord. Forgive me for laughing instead of having faith.

What problem seems impossible to you today?

Is Anything Too Hard?

But the LORD said to Abraham, "Why did Sarah laugh, saying, 'Shall I actually give birth to a child, when I am so old?' Is anything too difficult for the LORD? At the appointed time I will return to you, at this time next year, and Sarah will have a son."

GENESIS 18:13–14 NASB

Dear Father,

Is anything too difficult for You? The answer is no. Nothing is too hard for You, Father. Yet I find myself worrying, overcome with anxiety, afraid things won't work out the way I want them to. Help me take my hands off the situation, Lord. I worry because I want to be in control, but I'm not the right person to control any situation. I'd rather have You in the driver's seat, Lord. Teach me to relax in You, to trust Your goodness, and to say, "Nothing is too hard for my Father."

What situation are you trying to control?

God Is with You

At that time Abim'elech and Phicol the
commander of his army said to Abraham,
"God is with you in all that you do."
GENESIS 21:22 RSV

Dear Father,

Thank You for this reminder that when we live in Your will, when Your favor is on us, people notice. These men had watched Abraham, and they saw clearly that You were with Him. I know people watch me because they know I'm a Christian, and they want to see if You make a difference in my life. When I show worry and fear, I subconsciously tell others that I don't trust You. Mark me as Yours, Lord. Help me to live each day with such faith, such total trust, that others will know You are with me in all that I do.

When others watch your actions and listen to your
words, is there evidence that You belong to God?

God's Goodness

Before he had done speaking, behold, Rebekah, who was born to Bethu'el the son of Milcah, the wife of Nahor, Abraham's brother, came out with her water jar upon her shoulder. The maiden was very fair to look upon, a virgin, whom no man had known. She went down to the spring, and filled her jar, and came up.

GENESIS 24:15–16 RSV

Dear Father,

Why am I surprised at Your goodness? You didn't just provide Isaac with any girl. You brought him a beautiful young woman of appropriate age, with a similar background, to be his wife. She was generous and kind and pleasing in every way. Sometimes I make up my mind about what I want before consulting You. That's so silly, because I know what You have for me is far superior to what I might choose for myself. Forgive me for doubting Your goodness, Lord. Help me trust You with everything.

What do you need to trust God with today?

No Fear

There is no fear in love. But perfect love drives out fear, because fear has to do with punishment. The one who fears is not made perfect in love.

1 JOHN 4:18 NIV

Dear Father,

You are love. Time and again in Your Word, You reveal this truth. Time and again in my life, You've shown Your goodness. When I worry about things, when I let fear control my thoughts, I'm choosing to live outside of Your great love. It doesn't make any sense, yet I do it anyway. Forgive me for focusing on fear instead of sinking deep into Your perfect love. With You in control of my life, I have nothing to fear. Even when things don't go as I want them to, I can have confidence that Your plans for me are good. Help me to stay in Your perfect love.

What is your biggest fear right now?
How does that fear contrast to God's love for you?

Preparing the Way

When he saw the ring, and the bracelets on his sister's arms, and when he heard the words of Rebekah his sister, "Thus the man spoke to me," he went to the man; and behold, he was standing by the camels at the spring. He said, "Come in, O blessed of the LORD; why do you stand outside? For I have prepared the house and a place for the camels."

GENESIS 24:30–31 RSV

Dear Father,

Abraham sent his servant to find a wife for his son, Isaac. He wanted a young woman from his own people, who shared his faith. It must have seemed like a random, impossible task to the servant, to travel into this unknown-to-him land looking for an appropriate bride for his master's son. What if Isaac wasn't pleased? But when You send us on a journey, You always prepare the way, don't You, Father? Thank You for preparing the way for me.

What impossible task do you face today?

God's Best

Then Isaac brought her into the tent, and took
Rebekah, and she became his wife; and he loved her.
So Isaac was comforted after his mother's death.

GENESIS 24:67 RSV

Dear Father,

This is better than any Hallmark romance because it's
not fiction. It really happened. You didn't just provide any
woman for Isaac. You sent him a love match! In Rebekah,
You gave Isaac more than he could hope for. I know You have
wonderful things in store for my life as well. Why do I worry
that You'd give me the bare minimum when You're always so
generous? Sometimes I lower my standards because I don't
trust that You have something better for me. Forgive me for
ever settling for less than Your best for my life. Forgive me
for forgetting how lavish Your love is. Teach me to trust in
Your goodness, Your kindness, and Your love.

In what ways have you settled
for less than God's best for you?

Dig Another Well

*And he moved from there and dug another well, and
over that they did not quarrel; so he called its name
Reho'both, saying, "For now the LORD has made
room for us, and we shall be fruitful in the land."*

GENESIS 26:22 RSV

Dear Father,

Sometimes, for reasons that are out of our control, we have to start over. This has happened many times in my life, Lord. When that happens, I want to be like Isaac. He didn't waste time or breath lamenting how unfair life was. Instead, he just dug another well. He simply moved on, again and again, as many times as it took. Father, help me to move on from my past. Help me to dig another well, like Isaac did, again and again until I arrive at the place where You want me to stop. You blessed Isaac's perseverance, Lord. Give me strength to persevere too.

*From what circumstance do you need to move
forward? What new well do you need to dig?*

Giving Up Control

Jacob said to his father, "I am Esau your firstborn.
I have done as you told me; now sit up and eat
of my game, that your soul may bless me."
GENESIS 27:19 ESV

Dear Father,

Jacob lied to his father. But it goes much deeper than a lie. Rebekah, Jacob's mother, set up the farce. She was worried that things wouldn't go the way she thought they should, so she decided to help things along. You had promised her that Jacob would be blessed, but she didn't trust You.

How often have I done the same thing, Lord? Maybe I haven't encouraged my children to lie, but I've certainly tried to manipulate things to my advantage instead of trusting You with the outcome. If I'll just step back, have patience, and let You work, I know I'll save myself a lot of grief and heartache. Help me act in faith, Father.

What situation do you need to give to God today?

He Promised

"Behold, I am with you and will keep you wherever you go, and will bring you back to this land; for I will not leave you until I have done that of which I have spoken to you."

GENESIS 28:15 RSV

Dear Father,

You made this promise to Jacob despite all the low-down, manipulative things he did to his father and his brother. I know you make the same promise to me in spite of all my failures. When I'm tempted to worry about my future, bring these words to mind. I don't have to fear being alone because You will stay with me and keep me wherever I go. I don't have to be afraid that Your plans won't come to fruition. As long as I trust You and stay close to You, You will fulfill Your purpose in my life. Because You are good and loving and kind, I know my future is safe with You.

What about your future causes you the most anxiety? Can you trust God with it?

Hardships and Blessings

Before the year of famine came, Joseph had two sons,
whom As'enath, the daughter of Poti'phera priest of
On, bore to him. Joseph called the name of the first-
born Manas'seh, "For," he said, "God has made me
forget all my hardship and all my father's house."
The name of the second he called E'phraim, "For God
has made me fruitful in the land of my affliction."
GENESIS 41:50–52 RSV

Dear Father,

Joseph spent thirteen years from the time his brothers
put him in the pit until his rise to greatness. He had many
ups and downs. Help me remember to trust You when hard
times come. Help me to hang in there and be faithful. I know
You are good and that Your blessings are coming.

Are you in a season of blessing? Thank God
for your blessings. Are you in a season
of hardship? Trust Him for tomorrow.

Letting Go

"So it was not you who sent me here, but God; and he has made me a father to Pharaoh, and lord of all his house and ruler over all the land of Egypt."

GENESIS 45:8 RSV

Dear Father,

Joseph was able to forgive his brothers because he saw Your hand in all that had happened to him. I know much of my worry and anxiety often stems from not being able to let go of the past. Help me learn from Joseph's example. I know You don't cause bad things to happen to me, but sometimes You allow them so that they will propel me forward into a better future. Help me forgive others and let go of my past, knowing You are leading me into a future filled with Your promises and blessings.

Is there anyone you need to forgive? Is there something from your past you need to let go of?

Good Things to Come

When Jacob finished charging his sons, he drew up his feet into the bed, and breathed his last, and was gathered to his people. Then Joseph fell on his father's face, and wept over him, and kissed him.

GENESIS 49:33–50:1 RSV

Dear Father,

You were so gracious to Joseph to allow him to see his father, Jacob, again before he died. It had been so long, and Joseph could have easily lost hope of that ever happening. But You always have good things in store for those who love You, don't You, Father? When I'm tempted to lose hope, when I think nothing good will ever happen, remind me of this story and Your goodness. Help me to lay down my worry, because worry is simply a belief that bad things will happen. Hope is the belief that good things will come. Help me to hope in You.

How can you turn your worry into hope?

Letting Go

*"Fear not, for am I in the place of God? As for
you, you meant evil against me; but God meant
it for good, to bring it about that many people
should be kept alive, as they are today. So do not
fear; I will provide for you and your little ones."
Thus he reassured them and comforted them.*
GENESIS 50:19–21 RSV

Dear Father,

This passage is as much about forgiveness as it is about Your plan for us. Joseph would have carried so much anguish with him if he'd refused to forgive his brothers. He would have missed out on seeing his father again. He would have forfeited a future relationship with his brothers, including the younger brother he'd never met. I know when I refuse to forgive, it causes anxiety and stress to build up inside me. Help me to truly forgive those who have hurt me.

Whom do you need to forgive? Ask God to help you.

Milk and Honey

> *"I have come down to deliver them out of the
> hand of the Egyptians and to bring them up
> out of that land to a good and broad land,
> a land flowing with milk and honey."*
> EXODUS 3:8 ESV

Dear Father,

You promised Your people a land flowing with milk and honey. This promise was fulfilled in spite of their ongoing rebellion and disobedience. Why do I worry about things when I know You always have good things in store for those who love You? I know that worry really means I don't have faith in Your goodness. It means that, deep down, I struggle to believe Your promises. Forgive me for my lack of faith, Father. When I'm tempted to worry about the future, remind me of this land of milk and honey and of the good things You always have in store for Your children.

*What are some things on your "milk and honey" list?
Trust God for the good things He wants to give you.*

From Fear to Confidence

But Moses said to the LORD, "Oh, my Lord, I am not eloquent, either in the past or since you have spoken to your servant, but I am slow of speech and of tongue." Then the LORD said to him, "Who has made man's mouth?. . . Is it not I, the LORD?"

EXODUS 4:10–11 ESV

Dear Father,

I can so relate to Moses in this passage. There are things I want to do, things I feel You calling me to do, but I hesitate because I don't feel qualified. Thank You for this reminder to Moses that You created us, and You will qualify us to do the things You need us to do. Next time I feel anxious and unqualified, bring this passage to mind. Replace worry with confidence and fear with hope.

In what areas do you feel unqualified? How can you reframe your fears to reflect confidence in God?

43

God Restores

"I will restore to you the years that the swarming locust has eaten, the hopper, the destroyer, and the cutter, my great army, which I sent among you. You shall eat in plenty and be satisfied, and praise the name of the LORD your God, who has dealt wondrously with you."
JOEL 2:25–26 ESV

Dear Father,

Long before Joel penned these words, Moses led Your people out of bondage. You sent plagues of swarming locusts, among other things, to demonstrate Your power. Here, You promise Your people that even when we're devastated, even when all seems lost, You have the power to restore. Sometimes I look at the bad things that have happened in my past, and I project those events onto the future. Change my heart and my way of thinking, Lord. I know that no matter what's happened in the past, I can hope in Your goodness.

What would you like God to restore for you?

Even Your Enemies

The people of Israel had also done as Moses told them, for they had asked the Egyptians for silver and gold jewelry and for clothing. And the LORD had given the people favor in the sight of the Egyptians, so that they let them have what they asked. Thus they plundered the Egyptians.

EXODUS 12:35–36 ESV

Dear Father,

Thank You for this reminder that You can cause even our enemies to do nice things for us. Sometimes I worry about people who don't like me, and I lose sleep over those relationships. But I know when I walk with You, when I find favor with You, I also find favor in relationships. You can change people's hearts. Help me find favor even with those people who don't like me, Father. Help me to show them love and kindness in every situation. May my behavior reflect Your goodness and point them to You.

What relationships cause you concern?
Talk to God about them.

Talk about It

*Then Moses said to the people, "Remember this
day in which you came out from Egypt, out of
the house of slavery, for by a strong hand the
LORD brought you out from this place."*
EXODUS 13:3 ESV

Dear Father,

Just as the Israelites were commanded to remember and
talk about the good things You did for them, I know You want
me to do the same. When I remember Your goodness and
Your faithfulness to me in the past, I'm less likely to worry.
When I tell others about all the great things You've done
for me, it builds my faith. When I'm tempted to give in to
fear and anxiety, bring to mind all the amazing ways You've
shown Your love to me. Open doors for me to tell others
about Your greatness. Keep my focus on You, Lord, instead
of on my circumstances.

*What are three of the most amazing
things God has done for you?*

When It Doesn't Make Sense

When Pharaoh let the people go, God did not lead them by way of the land of the Philistines, although that was near. For God said, "Lest the people change their minds when they see war and return to Egypt." But God led the people around by the way of the wilderness toward the Red Sea. And the people of Israel went up out of the land of Egypt equipped for battle.

EXODUS 13:17–18 ESV

Dear Father,

Sometimes You do things that don't make sense to me at the time. But I know You always have a good reason for everything You take me through. In this passage, You wanted Your people to escape. You knew they'd become disheartened and return to bondage if they had to fight the Philistines, so You took them the long way around. Forgive me for doubting You when things don't make sense to me. I know Your ways are higher than my ways.

What in your life doesn't make sense right now?

Still and Silent

"The LORD will fight for you, and
you have only to be silent."
EXODUS 14:14 ESV

Dear Father,

I don't know why I fight so hard for things to go my way.
I try to maintain control when You only want me to be still.
You are already fighting my battles for me, and You do a
much better job than I can ever hope to do on my own. Help
me to stop worrying and complaining. Teach me to sit back
and watch You work, popcorn in hand, waiting to see what
great things You will do. I trust You, Father. Forgive me for
working and fighting and stressing out when all I need to do
is step aside, get out of Your way, and witness Your greatness
and glory in action.

*Have you been fighting your own battles? Practice
being still and silent today, and see what God does.*

Not Alone

Moses' father-in-law said to him, "What you are doing is not good. You and the people with you will certainly wear yourselves out, for the thing is too heavy for you. You are not able to do it alone."

EXODUS 18:17-18 ESV

Dear Father,

I must be a lot like Moses, trying to do everything alone. I don't know why I worry about things so much. Worry is my way of trying to maintain control, I guess. Thank You for the wisdom of Moses' father-in-law and for the reminder that we weren't meant to do life alone. You are always with me, fighting my battles, caring for me. When needed, You send others into my life to help. Forgive me for trying to work things out for myself. Help me to trust You with all my cares and concerns.

What things are you trying to do alone?
Give them to God today.

He Already Knows

All my longings lie open before you, Lord;
my sighing is not hidden from you.
PSALM 38:9 NIV

Dear Father,

You see my heart, don't You? You know every thought, every fear, every anxiety. When I sigh, You hear. When I cry, You feel every tear. You know how I struggle with worry. Lord, I want to give things to You. I want to let go and trust You with everything, but those thoughts just keep coming back. Help me to breathe in Your peace, breathe out my fear and anxiety. When worry takes over my thoughts, remind me that You've got it all under control. I know the struggle may continue, but right now, in this moment, I give it all to You. I trust You, Father. I lay it all down, open before You.

What worries plague you right now?
God already knows. Give them to Him.

Do Not Worry

*"Therefore I tell you, do not worry about your
life, what you will eat or drink; or about your
body, what you will wear. Is not life more than
food, and the body more than clothes?"*

MATTHEW 6:25 NIV

Dear Father,

The command not to worry is a hard one for me. I wish there were an on/off switch. I'd gladly turn off my anxiety permanently if I could. But every time I think I have a hold on my anxious thoughts, worry sneaks back in. The truth is, I know You'll take care of me. You always have. Even when bad things happen, You work them out for my ultimate good. I know the worry-free life is a discipline, and I have to work at it. Have patience with me, Lord, and teach me to let go. Teach me to soak in the peace You give to those who trust You completely.

*What physical things, such as food
and clothing, do you worry about?*

Blessable

*"Now therefore, if you will obey my voice and keep
my covenant, you shall be my own possession
among all peoples; for all the earth is mine."*

EXODUS 19:5 RSV

Dear Father,

That little word *if* holds such power. Here, you made a promise, but a condition is attached. You said You'd take care of things if Your people obeyed You. In other words, You'd bless them if they chose to be blessable. Sometimes I worry and fret about why things aren't going my way, when I should really be asking if I'm upholding my end of things. I know salvation doesn't come by works, but that does not negate my responsibility to obey You in all things. Thank You for Your promises and Your blessings, Lord. Help me to be obedient. I want to be blessable.

*How can you become more blessable today?
In what areas can you obey God better?*

Dwell Among Us

"I will dwell among the people of Israel, and will be their God. And they shall know that I am the LORD their God, who brought them forth out of the land of Egypt that I might dwell among them; I am the LORD their God."
EXODUS 29:45–46 RSV

Dear Father,

As I read this promise You made to dwell among the people of Israel, I want my family to be included. Please dwell among my people. Be our God. Just as You brought the Israelites out of bondage, You've brought us through so much. Keep my family, my friends, and all my loved ones close to You, Lord. Walk with us, stay in our thoughts, and guide us. For all the people in my circle who don't know You or aren't walking with You, draw them in, Father. Be our God. Mark us as Yours, and don't let us go.

Who are you worried about today? Call them by name, and ask God to stay close to them.

Prayer Changes Things

But Moses implored the LORD his God and said, "O LORD, why does your wrath burn hot against your people, whom you have brought out of the land of Egypt with great power and with a mighty hand? . . . Turn from your burning anger and relent from this disaster against your people.

EXODUS 32:11–12 ESV

Dear Father,

Thank You for this reminder that prayer changes things. You were angry at Your people for their continued disobedience. Even though they deserved punishment, You listened to Moses' pleas and changed Your plans. When I'm tempted to worry about things, bring this story to mind. My time is much better spent praying, talking to You, and asking You to change the course of things. You are gracious and good, merciful and kind, and You're always willing to listen to our cries for help. Father, thank You for not giving us what we deserve. Thank You for dealing with us with compassion and love.

Have you talked to God about what concerns you today?

Stepping Back

"Go up to a land flowing with milk and honey;
but I will not go up among you, lest I consume
you in the way, for you are a stiff-necked people."
EXODUS 33:3 RSV

Dear Father,

Sometimes I get angry and upset about things, and I don't handle it well. I explode or I hold it all inside, causing my anxiety to grow. When I'm upset, help me follow Your example. You were angry at Your people, and You stepped away for a while. You withdrew Your presence to give Yourself time to cool off so You wouldn't consume them with Your anger. Teach me to take a step back and give myself time to process instead of acting out my anxiety and frustration, doing and saying things I'll regret.

*What frustrations are building inside
you now? How can you take a step back
to avoid doing something you'll regret?*

Work, Not Worry

*According to all that the LORD had commanded
Moses, so the people of Israel had done all the
work. And Moses saw all the work, and behold,
they had done it; as the LORD had commanded,
so had they done it. And Moses blessed them.*

EXODUS 39:42-43 RSV

Dear Father,

I pray that at the end of my life, You'll survey all I've done and be pleased. When worry consumes me, I often become frozen. Anxiety keeps me from accomplishing the work You've planned for me. Set me free from the fear that paralyzes me, Father, so I can be a productive servant. I want to accomplish all the things You've set before me. With all that is in me, I want to please You.

*How has worry prevented you from doing what God has
called you to do? Ask God to deliver you from that fear.*

Waiting for the Cloud to Lift

Throughout all their journeys, whenever the cloud was taken up from over the tabernacle, the people of Israel would set out. But if the cloud was not taken up, then they did not set out till the day that it was taken up.

EXODUS 40:36-37 ESV

Dear Father,

So many of my fears increase when I move ahead of You. I decide how I want things to go, and I act without waiting for Your guidance. My actions often make things worse, not better, and my anxiety increases. Help me be like the Israelites, who waited for Your direction. The cloud being lifted from the tabernacle was Your sign that they should move forward. Oh, may I watch You that closely! May I never move at all until I'm sure You're showing me the way.

Have you moved in front of God lately?
Ask Him to clearly show you how and when to act.

The Fire

The fire on the altar shall be kept burning on it;
it shall not go out. The priest shall burn wood
on it every morning, and he shall arrange the
burnt offering on it and shall burn on it the fat of
the peace offerings. Fire shall be kept burning
on the altar continually; it shall not go out.
LEVITICUS 6:12–13 ESV

Dear Father,

The fire on the altar that never went out—that's a symbol of You, isn't it? It's a reminder that Your fire never goes out. No matter what's going on in my life, I can be confident that You're on it. Even when You seem distant, You're working on my behalf. Even when it looks like nothing is happening, You're changing circumstances, moving people's hearts, and making the way smooth for those who love You. Thank You for this reminder, Lord. Thank You that Your fire never ceases.

In what circumstances does it feel like God
isn't doing much? Trust that He's working.

Show Me Your Glory

And Moses said, "This is the thing that the
LORD commanded you to do, that the glory
of the LORD may appear to you."
LEVITICUS 9:6 ESV

Dear Father,

I love this reminder that You love obedience. When we obey You, You show up. When we obey You, You make Your presence known. Instead of worrying about things, I can simply do what You've commanded. I can love others, show kindness and mercy, and follow Your statutes. When I obey You, You'll stay close to me, and I'll see Your glory all around me. Forgive me for thinking I need to be in charge of my circumstances and make things happen my own way. When I'm tempted to struggle for control, remind me to simply obey You and watch for You to appear.

How can you obey God in your circumstances today?
Make a plan to do that, and watch for God to show up.

Be Holy

"For I am the LORD your God. Consecrate yourselves
therefore, and be holy, for I am holy. . . . For I am the
LORD who brought you up out of the land of Egypt to
be your God. You shall therefore be holy, for I am holy."
LEVITICUS 11:44–45 ESV

Dear Father,

Why do I so often forget that I was made in Your image?
Though I have a sin nature, I also have Your image running
through my veins. I was created to be like You, to be in
fellowship with You. The word *holy* means to set apart for
a high calling. When I allow fear and anxiety to rule my
thoughts, I'm not reflecting Your image or Your holiness.
When I'm tempted to worry, remind me that You've called
me to be holy, and worry isn't part of that picture.

In what ways can you reflect
God's holiness in your life today?

Like the Israelites

"Yet you would not go up, but rebelled against the
command of the LORD your God. And you murmured
in your tents and said, 'Because the LORD hated us
he has brought us out of the land of Egypt, to give
us into the hand of the Amorites, to destroy us.' "

DEUTERONOMY 1:26–27 ESV

Dear Father,

When I read about how ungrateful the Israelites were
for all You did for them, it's easy to be judgmental. But I'm
no different than they were, am I? When I think back over
my life, I recall so many ways You've shown Your love. You've
poured out Your mercy, Your compassion, Your kindness, and
still I worry. Worry is really just complaining in my head, isn't
it? Worry says that I don't trust Your goodness. Forgive me,
Lord. Today, right now, in this moment, I set aside my fear,
knowing You will take care of things in the best possible way.

What have you complained about recently?
Can you trust God with it?

In the Wilderness

"For the LORD your God has blessed you in all the work of your hands. He knows your going through this great wilderness. These forty years the LORD your God has been with you. You have lacked nothing."

DEUTERONOMY 2:7 ESV

Dear Father,

You have blessed me just as You blessed the Israelites. When I think back through my life, Your blessings are too many to count. You know all about the wilderness I'm going through, and You've never left me for a moment. You know every detail of every circumstance, and You've felt every tear I've cried. Every day, every hour of my life, You've been with me. Truly, I've never lacked a thing that I needed. Thank You, Lord, for Your constant, tender care over me. I love You. I trust You. I know You are good.

In what ways has God blessed you? How have you felt His presence in your own wilderness?

You Shall Not Fear

*"You shall not fear them, for it is the
LORD your God who fights for you."*
DEUTERONOMY 3:22 RSV

Dear Father,

If anyone had reason to worry, it was Joshua. His job was to bring the Israelites into a hostile land, and he knew they'd have to fight to possess the land You had promised them. But instead of worrying, he chose to recall all You'd done for Your people in the past. He knew You wouldn't bring them this far just to abandon them. He told the people not to worry for You were fighting for them. Help me follow Joshua's example, Lord. Help me make gratitude a daily practice, for I know recalling Your goodness is a key to overcoming worry. You've brought me through so much. Help me know, deep in my heart, that I have nothing to fear. I know You are fighting for me even now.

*In what ways has God fought for you in the past?
Trust that He's still fighting your battles.*

Tell of His Goodness

*"Only take care, and keep your soul diligently,
lest you forget the things that your eyes have
seen, and lest they depart from your heart all
the days of your life. Make them known to your
children and your children's children."*

DEUTERONOMY 4:9 ESV

Dear Father,

Recalling Your goodness in my life is a key to not worrying, isn't it? When I tell others about all the great things You've done for me, it helps everyone. It helps the listener to know and understand Your character. And it helps me by building my faith and renewing my confidence in Your great love. When worry claims my heart, remind me to talk about the things You've brought me through in the past. Thank You for Your unchanging, unfailing love, Father.

*What are some stories you can tell about
God's goodness? To whom can you tell them?*

His Steadfast Love

"For I the LORD your God am a jealous God, visiting the iniquity of the fathers on the children to the third and fourth generation of those who hate me, but showing steadfast love to thousands of those who love me and keep my commandments."

DEUTERONOMY 5:9-10 ESV

Dear Father,

I'm so honored to be a member of Your family, to be called Your child. I do love You, Lord, and I try to keep Your commandments. Because of this, I know I have nothing to fear. Even though I'm not perfect, You know my heart, and You promised to show steadfast, unfailing love to those who love You (that's me) and those who keep Your commandments (that's also me, to the best of my ability). Help me to rest in the confidence of Your never-ending, all-consuming love.

How can you demonstrate your love for God today?

A Heart Like This

"Oh that they had such a heart as this always, to fear me and to keep all my commandments, that it might go well with them and with their descendants forever!"
DEUTERONOMY 5:29 ESV

Dear Father,

Give me a heart like this, Lord. Instead of fearing my circumstances or my future or even other people, I only want to fear You. A better word for fear, in this case, is reverence. I want to be a God-fearing person. Help me to show You reverence, Lord, by keeping Your commandments and honoring You in all I do. I want to be counted among those who truly love You. I know You take care of those who sincerely obey and respect You. More than anything, I want to please You. Give me that kind of heart.

In what ways can you show God honor, reverence, and respect today?

Imperfect Love

"For you are a people holy to the LORD your God. The LORD your God has chosen you to be a people for his treasured possession, out of all the peoples who are on the face of the earth. It was not because you were more in number than any other people that the LORD set his love on you and chose you, for you were the fewest of all peoples."

DEUTERONOMY 7:6-7 ESV

Dear Father,

I know You don't bless us because we're righteous or because we deserve blessing. Our righteousness is like filthy rags to You (Isaiah 64:6). Instead, You bless those who love You—imperfect as that love may be—because You are good. You bless us because You keep Your promises. You bless us because You chose us. Help me to stop worrying, focus on loving You the best I can, and trust in Your goodness.

How can you show God you love Him today?

Good and Right

> *"Be careful to obey all these words that I command you, that it may go well with you and with your children after you forever, when you do what is good and right in the sight of the LORD your God."*
>
> DEUTERONOMY 12:28 ESV

Dear Father,

I know that when I worry and fret and become anxious over the future, I'm not focusing on what You want me to. Worry won't help my future a bit, but loving You and following Your commands will help set up my future for Your blessing. Help me shift my focus, Lord. Instead of thinking about how I can fix my own future, I need to simply do what is good and right in Your sight. Thank You for Your promise to care for those who love You.

*What things can you do today and every day
that are good and right in God's sight?*

Treasured

"For you are a people holy to the LORD your God, and the LORD has chosen you to be a people for his treasured possession, out of all the peoples who are on the face of the earth."

DEUTERONOMY 14:2 ESV

Dear Father,

How is it possible that You've chosen me? How is it that You consider me a treasured possession? According to this verse, You've selected me out of all the people on the face of the earth. If I am Your treasure, I know You'll take care of me. If I'm Your treasure, I don't have to worry about anything because You'll make sure I have everything I need—financially, physically, spiritually, and emotionally. Because I'm Your treasure, I know my anxieties and fears are nothing more than lies intended to steal my peace. Forgive me for doubting Your love for me. I trust You, Father. Thank You for choosing me.

How has God demonstrated that you're His treasured child?

God's Word

"And it shall be with him, and he shall read in it all the days of his life, that he may learn to fear the LORD his God by keeping all the words of this law and these statutes, and doing them."

DEUTERONOMY 17:19 ESV

Dear Father,

This verse shows me the importance of reading Your Word every single day. You commanded the kings of Israel to do this because Your Word gives wisdom for life. Your Word is a treasure, Lord. I have this treasure right at my fingertips, and yet too often, I don't choose to use it. Draw me to Your Word, Lord. Remind me each day to read it, to soak it in, to make it a part of me. Thank You for Your Word, Father.

Do you make daily Bible reading a habit? If not, how can you arrange your schedule to make God's Word a priority?

Purity and Strength

*"When you go forth against your enemies and are in
camp, then you shall keep yourself from every evil thing."*
DEUTERONOMY 23:9 RSV

Dear Father,

Evil weakens us. Sin destroys us. You tell us to avoid evil
because You want us to be strong. There is a battle going on
for my spirit, and I remain strong in that fight by remaining
pure. It's really hard to stay pure in this world, Lord. Evil seeps
in from every side, through every crack and crevice. The evil
around me causes my fears to flare, my anxieties to amplify.
But I know if I want to stand strong against the enemy, I must
remain pure. Help me to keep myself from evil and sin, for
I know purity equals strength. Move my focus from the evil
around me to the source of my strength: You.

*How have you focused on evil and negative things?
Shift your focus to your heavenly Father, who loves you.*

Circumcise Your Heart

"And the LORD your God will circumcise your heart and the heart of your offspring, so that you will love the LORD your God with all your heart and with all your soul, that you may live."
DEUTERONOMY 30:6 RSV

Dear Father,

Circumcision is a painful process. Its purpose is to cut away the excess so germs can't breed and cause infection. When You circumcise my heart, You're removing the excess, the things that can hide evil and impurity. It's a painful process but a necessary one to keep me pure and guard me against the effects of sin. I know that true life, true living, happens when I love You with all my heart and soul, and I love You best when I'm pure and clean from sin. Thank You for this reminder that You allow the painful things in my life to keep me pure, so I can live the best life possible.

How has God used painful events in your life to purify you?

Choose Life

*"I call heaven and earth to witness against
you this day, that I have set before you life and
death, blessing and curse; therefore choose life,
that you and your descendants may live."*

DEUTERONOMY 30:19 RSV

Dear Father,

I know I choose life—beautiful, abundant life—when I
choose to love and trust You with all my heart. I don't know
why I choose not to trust You sometimes. It's a constant battle
of faith versus fear. When I'm tempted to give in to anxiety,
remind me that I always have a choice. Though it may be a
struggle, I can force those anxious thoughts from my mind
and focus on You, on Your goodness, on Your kindness, and
on Your love. My default setting is often worry and fear, but I
can *choose* faith. Today and every day, I choose to trust You.

*In what ways can you choose abundant
life instead of worry and fear?*

Do Not Fear

"It is the LORD who goes before you; he will be with you, he will not fail you or forsake you; do not fear or be dismayed."
DEUTERONOMY 31:8 RSV

Dear Father,

Thank You for this reminder. I fear all the time. I feel dismayed all the time. I don't know why it's so hard for me to remember that You're with me. You're before me, behind me, and on either side. When I feel afraid, remind me of Your presence. In both Genesis and Revelation, You're called the Lion of Judah. Help me to picture You as a powerful Lion, walking with me wherever I go. With You as my guard, I have nothing to fear. I know You'll never fail me or forsake me. Thank You for being there, Father.

What situation leaves you feeling afraid and dismayed? Trust that God has it under control.

Encompass Us

Of Benjamin he said, "The beloved of the LORD, he dwells in safety by him; he encompasses him all the day long, and makes his dwelling between his shoulders."
DEUTERONOMY 33:12 RSV

Dear Father,

Make me Your beloved. Make each person in my family, each person I love, make us Your beloved. Encompass us all day long, and cause us to dwell in safety. When I'm tempted to worry about my children, my parents, my family members, and my friends, remind me that You are the One who keeps them safe, and Your care is worth a lot more than my worry. I give them to You, Father. I call each of them by name before You and ask that You hold them close in the palm of Your hand. Thank You for Your protection over those You love.

Who are you worried about today? Call them by name in prayer, and trust that God will protect them.

Strong and Courageous

"Only be strong and very courageous, being careful to do according to all the law that Moses my servant commanded you. Do not turn from it to the right hand or to the left, that you may have good success wherever you go."
JOSHUA 1:7 ESV

Dear Father,

I need to memorize this verse and quote it every time I feel anxious. You are with me wherever I go. You set Your bodyguards before me, behind me, and on either side. I have nothing to fear. Nothing can intimidate me. Through You and because of You, I am strong and courageous! Help me to play this verse on repeat in my mind and bring it forward whenever I'm tempted to fear. Thank You for these words, Father. Thank You for making me stronger and more courageous than I ever thought possible.

In what ways can you change your behavior to reflect strength and courage instead of fear?

Prepare Your Provisions

*"Pass through the camp, and command the people,
'Prepare your provisions; for within three days you are to
pass over this Jordan, to go in to take possession of the
land which the LORD your God gives you to possess.' "*

JOSHUA 1:11 RSV

Dear Father,

"Prepare your provisions." You simply wanted the people
to obey, to get ready for the great things You were about to
do. They didn't have to do any of it on their own. They just
had to be ready. I love this reminder that all You require is
my obedience. I don't have to be successful by the world's
standards. I don't even need to be particularly capable. You
only want my pure-hearted obedience as I wait expectantly,
ready for You to act.

*How can you "prepare your provisions" today?
How can you obey God in a way that shows you're
ready for Him to do something that only He can do?*

Blessed

Blessed is the man who walks not in the counsel of the wicked, nor stands in the way of sinners, nor sits in the seat of scoffers; but his delight is in the law of the LORD, and on his law he meditates day and night.

PSALM 1:1–2 RSV

Dear Father,

In Your Word, You direct us to stay away from evil, wicked people and stay close to You. When we do these things, You bless us. Teach me to avoid negative people, people who try to draw me in. Whether it's gossip and slander, negative talk, or something else, give me wisdom as I deal with these people. Show me how to treat them with love and respect but not to make them my close advisors and friends. At the same time, draw me into Your presence each day. Remind me to spend time reading Your Word and talking to You. When I'm close to You, I'm blessed by Your nearness.

What steps can you take to be blessed, according to these verses?

Tears

*I am weary with my moaning; every night I
flood my bed with tears; I drench my couch with
my weeping. My eye wastes away because of
grief, it grows weak because of all my foes.*

PSALM 6:6-7 RSV

Dear Father,

You have seen my tears. You've heard my cries. You know every thought, as if I've spoken them out loud. You know my fears, my anxieties. You know every detail of every situation that keeps me awake at night. And even though I know I should trust You more, I don't feel condemned by You. Instead, I feel Your compassion, Your kindness, Your love. I sense You holding me, wiping my tears, and rocking me in Your presence. Thank You for being there for me, Father. Thank You for loving me through my doubts and fears and worries. I'm so grateful that You are my God.

*What have you lost sleep and tears over? God knows.
He sees. And He longs to comfort you with His presence.*

Refuge

*O LORD my God, in thee do I take refuge; save me from
all my pursuers, and deliver me, lest like a lion they
rend me, dragging me away, with none to rescue.*

PSALM 7:1-2 RSV

Dear Father,

You are my refuge. You're my safe place from everything that pursues me, causes me to worry, and steals my sleep. Sometimes it's people who crank up my anxieties. Sometimes it's money, or work issues, or health concerns. I'm afraid they'll overcome me, Lord. But when I take a moment to remember who You are, my heart rate slows and my anxieties calm. Those problems are nothing compared to You! I know You love me more than I can fathom. With that kind of love, why do I ever doubt that You'll take care of me? Save me from the people and circumstances that pursue me, Father. I love and trust You with all my heart.

*Who or what do you feel is pursuing you right now?
Picture God standing between you and the circumstance.*

The Shield

My shield is with God, who saves the upright in heart. God is a righteous judge, and a God who feels indignation every day.

PSALM 7:10–11 ESV

Dear Father,

Sometimes I foolishly think You don't know what I'm going through. I worry and fret in my belief that bad things will happen if I don't somehow take control of the situation. But when I give myself a moment to breathe, when I take time to consider things, I remember who You are. You are my shield, Lord. You love and care for me not because of anything I've done but simply because I'm Yours. You are righteous and good, and when bad things happen to Your children, You are indignant. Thank You for this reminder that You know, You see, and You will protect me.

What are you going through right now? God already knows, and He sees everything that happens to you. He stands in front of you like a shield, ready to protect and defend you.

Give Thanks

*I will give thanks to the LORD with my whole heart; I will
tell of all thy wonderful deeds. I will be glad and exult
in thee, I will sing praise to thy name, O Most High.*

PSALM 9:1-2 RSV

Dear Father,

Thank You for all the amazing things You've done for me.
When my thoughts turn to worry and fear, remind me how
You've loved me, cared for me, and carried me through even
the most difficult of circumstances. Give me opportunities to
share the great things You've done in my life. I know when I
talk about Your goodness, it helps to focus my thoughts on
You and not on my anxieties. Like the verse says, I will tell of
Your wonderful deeds. I will be glad in You. I will sing praise
to Your name, oh Most High.

*What do you thank God for today?
Set your thoughts on those things.*

Far Away?

Why, O LORD, do you stand far away?
Why do you hide yourself in times of trouble?
PSALM 10:1 ESV

Dear Father,

Thank You for allowing me to question You. I know You welcome my honest conversations, my sincere inquiries about what's going on and how You're working. Sometimes, I just need to talk about my fears and frustrations, and it's a comfort to pour out my thoughts to You. When I talk to You in this way, Lord, I always walk away from the conversation feeling better, more at peace. Even though You don't always answer the way I want or on my timeline, I know You've heard my pleas, and You have it all under control. Even when You seem far away, when it feels like You're hiding, I know You're actively working on my behalf. I trust You.

Does it feel like God is far away?
Tell Him, and ask Him to show Himself.

How Long?

How long must I bear pain in my soul,
and have sorrow in my heart all the day?
How long shall my enemy be exalted over me?
PSALM 13:2 RSV

Dear Father,

According to some scholars and evidenced by the psalms, David struggled with depression. So many of the psalms are written from a broken, anguished heart. Yet in each of these, David comes back around to praising God. I've found the same to be true. When I sincerely pour out my heart to You, I find comfort and peace in Your presence. When I lift You up in prayer and praise, I get lifted up as well. I have pain in my soul today, Lord, and sorrow in my heart. But I know You are faithful and that Your love is never ending. Thank You for being so good to me, Father.

What pain and sorrow do you carry in
your heart right now? How has God shown
Himself faithful to you in the past?

God Is with Me

*There they shall be in great terror, for God
is with the generation of the righteous.*
PSALM 14:5 RSV

Dear Father,

Evil is all over the news. It's everywhere. Even when I try to shelter myself from the onslaught of negative media, it seeps in. I can't escape it. But I know that You are with the righteous. You are actively working for those who love You. One day, every evil deed will be called to account, and every person who has rejected Your ways will pay for the things they've done. Thank You for sending Jesus to pay for my sins, and thank You for being with me and protecting me, every step I take. Thank You for counting me among the righteous not because of my own deeds but because of what Christ did on the cross.

*Are you worried about evil in the world?
Trust that God will one day bring justice.*

Fullness of Joy

You make known to me the path of life;
in your presence there is fullness of joy;
at your right hand are pleasures forevermore.
PSALM 16:11 ESV

Dear Father,

You have so many good things in store for me. I can look back on my life and see Your fingerprints all over the place. In light of Your goodness, I don't know why I struggle with fear and anxiety. All I need to do is stay close to You, and Your joy will surround me. It's all about focus, isn't it? I can choose to see the sunset, or I can focus on the telephone wires that get in the way. I can look at fields of flowers, or I can home in on one dead tree. Make known to me the path of life and joy and peace, Lord. Draw my attention to all the beautiful gifts You've placed in my life for me to enjoy.

Where is your focus today?
Think of something good to dwell on.

Deliver Me

You delivered me from strife with the people;
you made me the head of the nations; people
whom I had not known served me.

PSALM 18:43 ESV

Dear Father,

It's easy to focus on the end result of this prayer without thinking about the beginning. You delivered David, but in order to be delivered, he had to go through some pretty rough things. If he hadn't, he wouldn't have needed saving. Father, I know the difficult things I go through are often necessary to shape me and change me into the person You want me to be. But I'm tired of all the strife, Lord. I'm anxious and scared and weary, and I need You to rescue me. Please deliver me like You delivered David. Let my end result be a place of peace, and let it come soon.

What is causing you strife today?
Ask God to deliver you from it.

God's Word

*The law of the LORD is perfect, reviving the
soul; the testimony of the LORD is sure, making
wise the simple; the precepts of the LORD are
right, rejoicing the heart; the commandment
of the LORD is pure, enlightening the eyes.*

PSALM 19:7-8 ESV

Dear Father,

I know Your Word is the most valuable learning tool
available to me. It's the most precious thing I can fill my mind
with. No news or television show, popular music, or bestselling
novel can compare. I know from experience that when I fill my
mind with Your thoughts and Your words, my anxiety decreases.
Draw me to Your Word, Lord. Remind me to spend time with
You each day. Protect my time and my schedule so nothing
can crowd You out, Lord. You are my priority.

*Are you in the habit of spending time each
day reading God's Word? If not, what can
you do to make that a priority?*

In God I Trust

*Some trust in chariots and some in horses, but
we trust in the name of the LORD our God. They
collapse and fall, but we rise and stand upright.*

PSALM 20:7-8 ESV

Dear Father,

In David's time, people trusted in a mighty army with the best chariots and horses to keep them safe. The better the military forces, the lower the anxiety. Today, I might be tempted to trust in our military as well. I also might trust in my bank account, my job, my family, my friends, or any number of things. But I know any of these people or things may fail me at any moment. You are the only constant. You are the only One in my life who will never fail. I trust in You alone for everything I need.

*Other than God, what are you tempted to
trust in for your safety and well-being?
How is God better than those things?*

God's Address

Yet you are holy, enthroned on the praises of Israel.
PSALM 22:3 ESV

Dear Father,

Sometimes I feel so far from You. I look for You, but it seems like You're hiding. Thank You for this verse, which reveals Your personal address. You live in the praises of Your people! When You feel far away, all I need to do is praise You, and there You'll be. When I feel worried and stressed, anxious and afraid, Your praise will bring You near. Father, I praise You right now, in this moment. You are amazing, awesome, wonderful, beautiful. You are more than I can ever think or imagine, and I'm so humbled and grateful to be allowed into Your presence. Thank You for making me Your child and for always being within my reach.

When is the last time you dedicated a specific amount of time to simply praise God? Do that today.

He Restores

The LORD is my shepherd; I shall not want.
He makes me lie down in green pastures. He leads
me beside still waters. He restores my soul. He leads
me in paths of righteousness for his name's sake.

PSALM 23:1-3 ESV

Dear Father,

You restore. This indicates hardship, because why would You restore something that doesn't need restoration? I know You will restore my dry, thirsty soul. Later in this chapter, it says, "Surely goodness and mercy shall follow me all the days of my life." When I'm tempted to worry, remind me of these promises, Lord. You will restore what's been lost. You will send goodness and mercy to pursue me. Thank You for the confidence I can have in Your love for me and in Your restorative power over my life.

What do you need God to restore
for you? Talk to Him about it now.

Wait on God

Indeed, none who wait for you shall be put to shame;
they shall be ashamed who are wantonly treacherous.

PSALM 25:3 ESV

Dear Father,

When I'm patient and wait on Your timing, it always pays off. But when I carelessly act on my own, that's when disaster strikes. Help me to calm down and wait on You. I know I need to stop trying to control my circumstances. I need to stop trying to force things to happen in my own way, my own time. Your plan is so much better than anything I can bring about on my own. Teach me to be calm and simply rest in Your love, Father, as I wait for You to act according to Your will. I love You and trust You, and I will wait on Your timing.

Are you trying to control a circumstance
instead of waiting on God? Step back,
take a deep breath, and trust His timing.

Holy Reverence

Who is the man who fears the LORD? Him will
he instruct in the way that he should choose.
PSALM 25:12 ESV

Dear Father,

I fear You... not because You are unkind but because You are powerful. This kind of fear is really reverence. I revere You, Father, and I want to please You. Your Word says that when we fear You with a holy reverence, You will show us which way to go. You'll direct our paths and assist us in our decisions. Instead of worrying about things, I know I just need to honor You with my life and listen to Your Holy Spirit's guidance. Help me, Father, to follow Your instruction instead of trying to figure things out on my own. I trust Your timing.

Do you need God's help in your decisions? Spend some
time in sincere, reverent prayer, and listen for His guidance.

I Wait

*Oh, guard my soul, and deliver me! Let me not be
put to shame, for I take refuge in you. May integrity
and uprightness preserve me, for I wait for you.*

Psalm 25:20–21 esv

Dear Father,

There is that word again: wait. I am waiting for You,
Father. It seems I've waited for such a long time. Please deliver
me from the circumstances that worry my heart, plague my
mind, and steal my sleep. You are my refuge, my safe place.
Let me feel Your presence, Lord, and let me see You working.
I know You are the only One who can change the trajectory of
my life. You have the power to change relationships, finances,
even people's hearts. I'm waiting, Lord, knowing You will work
in Your time. Please let it be soon.

*In what circumstance are you waiting for God to act?
Remember, even when we can't see progress, He is working.*

So Many Stories

Proclaiming thanksgiving aloud,
and telling all your wondrous deeds.
PSALM 26:7 ESV

Dear Father,

There are reasons You tell us to talk about all the great things You've done. When we share with others how You've brought us through difficult things in the past, those who hear are drawn to You. It also sets our minds on Your mighty works instead of on our fears. Finally, praising You causes You to lean close, drawing near to Your children. Make me bold to tell others about all the amazing things You've done and continue to do in my life. There are so many stories to tell; the most wondrous is the story of my salvation. I can think of so many other things You've done for me, Father. I don't know why I ever worry about anything. You have proven Yourself to be good and kind, gracious and merciful, time and again.

What are some of your favorite stories about God's
goodness in your life? Thank God for them now.

Active Faith

*I believe that I shall look upon the goodness of the LORD
in the land of the living! Wait for the LORD; be strong,
and let your heart take courage; wait for the LORD!*
PSALM 27:13–14 ESV

Dear Father,

You want me to wait. While I wait, You want me to have sturdy faith. The writer of this psalm believed, without doubt, that he would see good things in this life, while he was still alive. Job reflected the same kind of faith in the midst of the worst trials imaginable. I want that kind of faith, Father. I know faith is an action more than a feeling. It's a decision to push aside all worry and doubt and fear in favor of a belief in Your goodness. Sometimes, shoving that worry aside feels like a physical task. It's heavy and stubborn. But with all my strength, I will practice faith. I will believe in Your kindness with expectation, and I'll wait, knowing good things will come.

How can you practice faith today?

Praise and Fear

Blessed be the Lord! For he has heard the voice of my pleas for mercy. The Lord is my strength and my shield; in him my heart trusts, and I am helped; my heart exults, and with my song I give thanks to him.

PSALM 28:6-7 ESV

Dear Father,

I love these psalms that are so filled with positive thinking. Worry and fear cannot coexist with praise and thanksgiving. I want to add my voice to the psalmist's and bless You! Thank You for always hearing my prayers. Thank You for jumping at my cries for help and coming to my rescue. You truly are my strength, getting me through the most difficult times. You are my shield, surrounding and protecting me physically, spiritually, and emotionally. I trust You, I praise You, and I thank You for every good thing. I love You with my whole heart.

For what do you praise God today?
When fear sets in, praise will push it out.

King of My Life

The LORD sits enthroned over the flood;
the LORD sits enthroned as king forever.
PSALM 29:10 ESV

Dear Father,

You truly are King over everything. You rule over every place, every time, every circumstance. When good things happen, You get the credit. When bad things happen, You see, and You work to bring about justice. This verse says You're enthroned over the flood, which means You are enthroned over things that can seem threatening and scary. Just as You used the flood in the Old Testament to bring about Your perfect plan, I know You use the frightening, uncomfortable circumstances in my life to make me stronger, more resilient, and more like You. Thank You for being the King of my life and for reigning over every detail.

Over what circumstance do you need to acknowledge
God as King? Picture Him on His throne, reigning
over every aspect of that circumstance.

Sing Praises

Sing praises to the LORD, O you his saints, and give thanks to his holy name. For his anger is but for a moment, and his favor is for a lifetime. Weeping may tarry for the night, but joy comes with the morning.

PSALM 30:4-5 ESV

Dear Father,

Thank You for this reminder that although not everything in my life is perfect or happy, those difficult times are only temporary. Though some circumstances bring a flood of tears, I will eventually find relief. I know You love me. I'm Your child, and You don't want me to hurt forever. Though things may seem desperate and impossible right now, I know nothing is impossible with You. You are the God of hope, and You will surely send joy in the morning. Even in the middle of the storm, I'll praise You and thank You. And I'll wait expectantly, knowing You have good things in store.

What is the most difficult circumstance in your life right now? Hang in there. Joy is on its way.

Be Gracious to Me

Be gracious to me, O LORD, for I am in distress;
my eye is wasted from grief; my soul and my
body also. For my life is spent with sorrow, and
my years with sighing; my strength fails because
of my iniquity, and my bones waste away.

Psalm 31:9–10 esv

Dear Father,

Just as David cried out to You, so do I. Deliver me, Lord. Deliver my children, my spouse, my loved ones, my friends. Heal us of pride, stubbornness, laziness, selfishness, fear, anxiety, and anything else that stands in the way of Your perfect plan for our lives. These traits are our adversaries, stronger than any human opponent, and we need Your help. Turn our hearts to You, and help us trust You. Mature us and draw us daily into Your presence. Hear my cries for myself, my family, my friends, Lord. Be gracious and deliver us.

What keeps you awake at night?
Talk to God about it today. Tell Him what's
on your heart, and ask Him for deliverance.

Stop the Silence

For when I kept silent, my bones wasted away
through my groaning all day long. For day and
night your hand was heavy upon me; my strength
was dried up as by the heat of summer.
PSALM 32:3-4 ESV

Dear Father,

I don't know why I'm prone to hold things in. When I keep my sin, my fear, my anxiety inside, it destroys me. It's like an infection that slowly spreads through my body; it zaps my strength and steals my sleep. Today I want to confess, Lord. Everything that's in me that doesn't please You, expose it, Lord. Bring it to the surface. I'm sorry for all my sins. I'm sorry for my anger, my bitterness, my lack of forgiveness to others. I'm sorry for my lack of faith. I don't want to keep silent anymore, Father. It feels good to get it all out in the open and leave it with You.

What do you need to confess today? Tell Him.

Wait

*Our soul waits for the LORD; he is our help
and our shield. For our heart is glad in him,
because we trust in his holy name.*

PSALM 33:20-21 ESV

Dear Father,

Why do You tell us so many times in scripture to wait? You must know how prone we are to impatience. Am I trying to move ahead of You in some situation? If so, hold me back, Lord. Calm my spirit and help me to just rest in the confidence that You are working on my behalf even when I don't see or feel it. Trust is hard for me, Lord, and I'm sorry for that. I have no reason to doubt Your faithfulness, Your goodness, or Your love. Today, when I try to step in front of You and force things to happen the way I want them to, whisper a reminder to trust You, to rest in Your love for me, and to wait.

In what situation are you waiting on God?

Hope in You

Let your steadfast love, O LORD,
be upon us, even as we hope in you.
PSALM 33:22 ESV

Dear Father,

I love the word *hope*. It is the belief that something good will happen. It's the opposite of fear, which is the belief that bad things are coming. Your Word tells me again and again that You are the God of hope and that fear is from Satan. When I let myself be ruled by anxiety, I'm really saying that I believe Satan is more powerful than You are. I don't mean to do that. Satan is really good at his game, and he knows how to feed my fears. Give me strength to resist his lies and to stand strong in hope. I love You, I trust You, and I know You are good.

In what situation are you struggling for hope?
Trust in God's goodness today, knowing He
loves you and He's working on your behalf.

Keys to Life

What man is there who desires life and loves many days, that he may see good? Keep your tongue from evil and your lips from speaking deceit. Turn away from evil and do good; seek peace and pursue it.

PSALM 34:12-14 ESV

Dear Father,

So many of my fears and anxieties stem from wanting to live a good, long, prosperous life. But what good is a long life if it's filled with worry? You've given me all the keys to have a good, successful life. In 2 Timothy 1:7, Your Word tells me that fear is not from You. Instead, You give power and love and a sound mind. Here, You've told me to keep my mouth closed to negative things, turn away from evil and do good, and seek peace and chase after it. Thank You for such a specific list, Father. Help me as I take action to live a life that pleases You.

What things on this list of life-giving actions will you pursue today?

Delight in Him

*Let those who delight in my righteousness shout
for joy and be glad and say evermore, "Great is the
LORD, who delights in the welfare of his servant!"*

PSALM 35:27 ESV

Dear Father,

Your righteousness is truly a delight. When I worry about things, I know I'm not focusing on Your goodness but on Satan's lies. When I worry, I'm succumbing to the belief that You're not good, You're not righteous, and that I'm doomed. That's not how I want to live my life. Forgive me for the negative thought patterns I've allowed to rule me, and heal me of them, Father. Whenever those bad thoughts show up, help me shove them aside and focus on Your goodness, Your righteousness, and Your faithfulness. I know You delight in doing good things for me, and I trust in Your love.

*Do you delight in God's righteousness?
Spend time today thinking about all the
good things He's done for you and others.*

Overwhelming Goodness

Your steadfast love, O LORD, extends to the heavens, your faithfulness to the clouds. Your righteousness is like the mountains of God; your judgments are like the great deep; man and beast you save, O LORD.

PSALM 36:5-6 ESV

Dear Father,

I love the poetic beauty of these verses. But more than just beautiful language, these words are true. Your goodness is beyond measure. Sometimes worry and fear drop over me like a thick fog. Anxiety blocks my vision so I can't see You clearly. Remove the fog, Lord. Silence the lies. When they show up, let me hear these words louder, more clearly in my mind: Your love is higher than the heavens, and Your faithfulness reaches to the clouds. Your righteousness is taller than the highest mountains, and Your wisdom is deeper than the ocean. You save Your children because You love us. Thank You for Your overwhelming, everlasting goodness.

How has God proven His love to you in the past? Remember, His love never changes.

Delight

The steps of a man are established by the LORD, when he delights in his way; though he fall, he shall not be cast headlong, for the LORD upholds his hand.

PSALM 37:23-24 ESV

Dear Father,

Thank You for this promise. Instead of worrying about things, I can rest easy in the knowledge that You will prepare the way for me as long as I delight in You. My mind cannot focus on anxiety and praise at the same time. When my fears creep in and threaten to take hold of my thoughts, remind me to delight in You. Remind me to set my eyes on all the good things You have done, on Your faithfulness and strength and love. Help me find joy in You instead of finding fear in Satan's lies. I commit to spending time with You each day, reading Your Word, talking to You, and thinking about You. Hold my hand today, Lord, and keep me from stumbling into fear.

What aspect of God's goodness will you delight in today?

Faith in Training

For the LORD loves justice; he will not forsake his saints. They are preserved forever, but the children of the wicked shall be cut off. The righteous shall inherit the land and dwell upon it forever.

PSALM 37:28–29 ESV

Dear Father,

I believe this in my head. Why is it so hard to believe it in my heart? You love me, and You will never, ever forsake those who love You. One way I show my love to You is simple faith. Hebrews 11:6 says that without faith, it's impossible to please You. Yet when I succumb to worry and fear, I'm not exhibiting faith. My faith may be weak at times, Lord, but I want to exercise to make it stronger. Today, when I'm tempted to worry about things, remind me that I'm in training, building faith-muscle. Help me to heft aside my fears and grip on to faith in Your goodness, Your mercy, and Your love.

How will you exercise faith today?

Crying Out

Do not forsake me, O LORD! O my God, be not far from me! Make haste to help me, O Lord, my salvation!

PSALM 38:21-22 ESV

Dear Father,

It's comforting to know that David struggled with fear and anxiety too. His desperation is clear in these verses. He's not resting peacefully, trusting You. Instead, He's crying out to You, and his worry is clear. I love it that You don't get angry at me for worrying. Instead, You want me to bring it to You. When anxiety crowds in, remind me to take it to You again and again and exchange it for Your peace. Help me do this as many times as it takes to rid myself of the weight. Like David, I know You'll never forsake me, but sometimes it's hard not to be afraid. In my fear, I cry out to You, knowing You're the only One who can save me and trusting that You will.

Have you cried out to God today? Do it now.

Measure My Days

> "O Lord, make me know my end and what is the
> measure of my days; let me know how fleeting
> I am! . . . Surely a man goes about as a shadow!
> Surely for nothing they are in turmoil; man heaps
> up wealth and does not know who will gather!"
>
> PSALM 39:4, 6 ESV

Dear Father,

Why do I worry about wealth, success, or status? What does it matter, anyway? I am but a wisp in the wind. May my wisp of time please You. May my short vapor of a life bring a brief moment of delight to Your heart. That's all I exist for, Abba Father. Forgive me for focusing on the things that don't matter and won't make a difference in light of eternity. Pleasing You is all that matters. Help me set my mind on loving You, loving others, and doing the good things You have planned for me to do.

What can you focus on today that will last for eternity?

In the Flood

Deep calls to deep at the roar of your waterfalls;
all your breakers and your waves have gone over me.
By day the LORD commands his steadfast love, and at
night his song is with me, a prayer to the God of my life.
PSALM 42:7–8 ESV

Dear Father,

Surely the author of this psalm understood anxiety and depression. I can so relate to the feeling of drowning described here. Yet the psalmist didn't remain focused on the breakers and waves washing over him. Instead, he turned to You, singing to You, searching for and feeling Your steadfast love. When worry floods my soul, help me follow this example. I will think of your steady, unfailing love for me. I will sing to You and pray to You. Instead of focusing on my problems, I will focus on You alone.

What is your favorite praise song? Sing it now.

When God Hides

Why do you hide your face? Why do you forget our affliction and oppression? For our soul is bowed down to the dust; our belly clings to the ground. Rise up; come to our help! Redeem us for the sake of your steadfast love!
PSALM 44:24–26 ESV

Dear Father,

As I read this author's words, I identify with the desperation he felt. He doesn't understand why things are so hard. Sometimes it feels like You've forgotten about me, Lord. I feel so low, like things can't get any worse. Please help me! Show me Your face. Let me feel Your presence, Father. I know You love me. I just need a visible reminder of that love. I'm desperate and shaken and anxious. I'm begging You. . . show Yourself to me now.

Have you ever felt like God is hiding? Call out to Him now, and watch for Him to make an appearance.

Problems Like Mountains

*God is our refuge and strength, a very present help
in trouble. Therefore we will not fear though the earth
gives way, though the mountains be moved into the
heart of the sea, though its waters roar and foam,
though the mountains tremble at its swelling.*

PSALM 46:1-3 ESV

Dear Father,

You are my refuge. When I'm afraid, You're my hiding place. You're also my strength. When I feel weak, like I just can't take another step, You give me the energy and the courage to move forward. Because of this, I will not fear. Though everything in my life may go wrong, though my problems seem like immovable mountains, though I feel like I'll be crushed any moment by an avalanche of my circumstances, I will trust You. I know with certainty that You are stronger than my fears, more powerful than my problems.

*What problems feel like they'll crush
you? God is bigger. Trust Him.*

Unmovable

God is in the midst of her; she shall not be moved;
God will help her when morning dawns.

PSALM 46:5 ESV

Dear Father,

I know this verse isn't talking about an actual woman. It's talking about Your holy city. Still, as I read it, I like to think it's talking about me. It could be. After all, You are in the midst of me. You live inside my heart, and You shall not be moved. Since my strength comes from You, I'm just as solid and steadfast as You in me. I know You'll help me when evening falls and when morning dawns and every moment in between. Every time I feel overcome with worry and anxiety, fear and depression, remind me of this verse, and remind me of its truth in my life.

Do you feel immovable? Spend some time
thinking about God's power living inside you.

Be Still

"Be still, and know that I am God. I will be exalted
among the nations, I will be exalted in the earth!"
PSALM 46:10 ESV

Dear Father,

So much of my worry is paired with restlessness, a need
to act, to do something when there's nothing that can be done.
But acting on my own, without Your prompting, shows a lack
of trust in Your sovereignty. Instead of trying to control things
in a nervous frenzy of activity, You've called me to simply
be still. To be quiet. To rest in the knowledge that You don't
need me or anyone else. You are all-powerful, and You have
everything under control. Forgive me for my agitation and
impatience. Each time I'm tempted to fill up my days with
nervous energy, shush my spirit. Quiet my soul. Remind me
to lay my head on Your great shoulder and simply, calmly
rest in You.

*Have you taken time to be still
and rest in God's presence today?*

Cattle on a Thousand Hills

"For every beast of the forest is mine, the cattle on a thousand hills. I know all the birds of the hills, and all that moves in the field is mine."

Psalm 50:10–11 esv

Dear Father,

Your power and resources are limitless. Too often, I view You by my own limitations, and I forget how formidable You are. I know You have more than enough of everything I need, whether it's money, food, relationships, good health, or something else. You are the generous Provider, and You will take care of everything in my life. I know it's silly that I worry about things I'm certain You will supply, but my mind quickly forgets. Help me to become more disciplined, to train my brain toward trust instead of worry. I know You will take care of me, Father.

What do you need God to provide for you?
Talk to Him about it. He won't let you down.

Saying Thanks

"The one who offers thanksgiving as his sacrifice glorifies me; to one who orders his way rightly I will show the salvation of God!"

PSALM 50:23 ESV

Dear Father,

When I'm overcome with worry and fear, thanksgiving really is a sacrifice. But I know thanksgiving is also the cure to my anxiety. When times get hard, I need to thank You! I need to praise You for the countless good things You've done in my life and in the lives of others. I need my thoughts to live in that place of gratitude instead of fear. Right now, in this moment, I want to express my thanks. You have never let me down. Time and again, You've poured out Your lovingkindness on me. You are good and gracious and generous beyond comprehension, and I love You.

What do you thank God for today?
Make a list. Nothing is too small or insignificant.

Through the Storms

*Be merciful to me, O God, be merciful to me, for in you
my soul takes refuge; in the shadow of your wings I will
take refuge, till the storms of destruction pass by.*

PSALM 57:1 ESV

Dear Father,

I know that nothing bad comes from You. You are
only love, and You are only good. But sometimes I wonder
if You allow some bad things into my life because of my
tendency to wander from You. When things are good, I often
become complacent in spending time with You. But when
circumstances bring worry and strife, I run to You. I know
You created me to have fellowship with You, and when I don't
spend time with You, You miss me. Forgive me for neglecting
You, Father. Have mercy on me as I hide in Your arms. Please
calm the storms, and help me stay close to You even when
things are good.

*What storms are you going through?
Ask God for mercy in the storms.*

Sing Loud!

But I will sing of your strength; I will sing aloud of your steadfast love in the morning. For you have been to me a fortress and a refuge in the day of my distress. O my Strength, I will sing praises to you, for you, O God, are my fortress, the God who shows me steadfast love.

PSALM 59:16–17 ESV

Dear Father,

Life brings difficult things. There's no way around it. When sin entered the world, along came hardship and trials. But as I look back on my life, it's the trials that have brought me closer to You. You've used those things to make me stronger, more compassionate, more gracious. Like David, I will sing loudly of Your steadfast love. I'll sing in the morning, at night, and in the middle of the day. No matter what I've gone through, You've been there. Thank You for loving me through it all, Father.

What is your song of praise today?
Sing it loudly, even if it's inside your head.

I Can't Save Myself

Oh, grant us help against the foe, for vain is the
salvation of man! With God we shall do valiantly;
it is he who will tread down our foes.

PSALM 60:11–12 ESV

Dear Father,

"For vain is the salvation of man." I can't save myself, Lord, no matter how hard I try. I need Your help. I know with You, mountains get moved. Problems get solved. Diseases are healed, and finances are replenished. Whatever comes against me, whether it's a person or a circumstance, will not win as long as You are on my side. I'm helpless without You, Father, but with You all things are possible. Please take over my circumstances. I'm desperate for You to save me. You're the only one who can.

In what circumstances have you tried to save yourself
without God's help? How did that work out? Ask
God to intervene, and then trust Him to act.

Not Greatly Shaken

For God alone my soul waits in silence; from him comes my salvation. He alone is my rock and my salvation, my fortress; I shall not be greatly shaken.

PSALM 62:1–2 ESV

Dear Father,

Once again, here's a reminder to wait. Worry and waiting can't coexist, because when I worry, I'm fidgety and I want to do something. When I wait in faith, I'm calm and I trust You. I love the last phrase of this passage: I shall not be greatly shaken. I don't like being shaken, Father. I want everything to be peaceful all the time. But without tension, any story is a dull one. You want me to live a grand adventure, which requires shaking things up now and then. You didn't say I won't be shaken at all. Rather, You said I won't be greatly shaken. Sometimes life may rattle me, but You won't allow any permanent damage. Thank You for Your perfect care over my life.

What has shaken you recently?
Trust that it won't destroy you.

Cling

For you have been my help, and in the shadow
of your wings I will sing for joy. My soul clings
to you; your right hand upholds me.

PSALM 63:7–8 ESV

Dear Father,

I cling to You. Like a frightened child clings to her parent, I cling to You. It's dark in my world right now, and I'm afraid, but I'll hold on to You with all my strength. I will sing praises to You, Father, in the midst of the storm. Though the tornado may drown out my song, I know You can still hear it. And even when I grow weary, when my grip starts to loosen, I know You have me. You have always had me, and You've never let me down. I love You. I praise You. And I know You are good.

Are you clinging tightly to God, or is your grip
loose right now? It's okay. Either way, He's got you.

Hemmed In

*Let the righteous one rejoice in the LORD and take
refuge in him! Let all the upright in heart exult!*
PSALM 64:10 ESV

Dear Father,

I know I am righteous not because of anything I've done
but because of what Christ did for me. Because of that gift
of salvation, I'm in right standing with You, and that's what
righteous means. Because I am in right standing with You, I
don't have to worry about anything. You have my back. You
also have my front and my sides. You hem me in, protecting
me from all directions. Even when I don't feel Your presence,
even when it seems like You're not there at all, I know You're
working on my behalf. I will rejoice in the knowledge that You
will never lose sight of me, and You're always protecting me.

*Have you ever pictured God standing in front of
you, behind you, and on either side, fighting off
enemies? Close your eyes and picture that now.*

Near God

But for me it is good to be near God; I have made the
Lord GOD my refuge, that I may tell of all your works.
PSALM 73:28 ESV

Dear Father,

   You are truly my refuge. Some things in my life are crazy
and scary, but I know You are with me. You have blessed me
in more ways than I can count. I know even when it seems
like wicked people and circumstances are prospering, You
are always in control. When I worry, I get distracted and
wander from Your presence. I don't want to do that, Lord. I
want to stay close to You. I want my heart and mind to remain
so focused on You that I don't even notice the storms around
me. I love You. Like the psalmist, I want to tell everyone about
how amazing You are.

At what time in your life did you feel closest to God?

So They Will Know

*That they may know that you alone, whose name is
the LORD, are the Most High over all the earth.*
PSALM 83:18 ESV

Dear Father,

You know everything that's going on in my life right now.
You know all the circumstances, all the details. And You know
exactly what they're doing to me. All the fear, the worry, the
anxiety. . . You know it all. I'm begging You, Father. Please
act. Please make Yourself known in this situation, in my life.
Deliver me and my loved ones from these circumstances in a
way that brings You glory so people will know You are God.
Just as You delivered Daniel from the lions' jaws, just as You
delivered Shadrach, Meshach, and Abednego from the fire,
please deliver me. I know You are able. Please show off so
everyone will know You are Most High.

*Do you believe God is able to deliver you from the
things you're worried about? Do you believe He will?*

Strength to Strength

Blessed are those whose strength is in you, in whose heart are the highways to Zion. As they go through the Valley of Baca they make it a place of springs; the early rain also covers it with pools. They go from strength to strength; each one appears before God in Zion.

PSALM 84:5-7 ESV

Dear Father,

Right now, I don't feel strong. In myself, I feel weak. But the blessings aren't found in my own strength. Instead, this passage says, "Blessed are those whose strength is in You." The "Valley of Baca" mentioned here is translated the "Valley of Weeping." That's where I am, Father. But when we're in the middle of that valley of weeping, You turn those tears into flowing, soothing springs. You cause Your children to go from strength to strength or to never grow weary. Give me Your strength, Father. I need You now.

In what areas do you feel weak right now?
Trust God alone for your strength.

Every Day

I am shut in so that I cannot escape; my eye grows dim through sorrow. Every day I call upon you, O LORD; I spread out my hands to you.

PSALM 88:8-9 ESV

Dear Father,

I can't escape from my fears, from the thoughts that plague my mind day and night. Like the psalmist, my eyes grow dim from sorrow. I feel desperate and hopeless, like nothing will ever get better. But I know those feelings aren't based on truth, Father, for You are the God of hope. With You, there is always the assurance of good things to come. So here I am, Lord. Every day, I call on You. Every day, I reach for You. And every day, I will find hope in You alone.

What fears plague you right now? Tell God about them every day. Rest in the knowledge that He knows, He loves you, and He is working on your behalf.

Because I'm Yours

*"Because he holds fast to me in love, I will deliver him;
I will protect him, because he knows my name. When
he calls to me, I will answer him; I will be with him in
trouble; I will rescue him and honor him. With long
life I will satisfy him and show him my salvation."*

PSALM 91:14–16 ESV

Dear Father,

What a comforting scripture this is. You don't love me
because of anything I've done. You love me because I belong
to You. I hold fast to You like a child to its parent. I call out
to You like a frightened toddler, afraid of the dark, and You
come right away. You won't ever leave me alone in my troubles.
Instead, You're right here, rescuing me, setting me in a high,
safe place, and pouring out Your love to me. Thank You for
loving me like this.

*Are you holding fast to God in love? Each time you
call His name aloud or in your thoughts, He is there.*

Flourish

*The righteous flourish like the palm tree and grow like
a cedar in Lebanon. They are planted in the house
of the L ORD; they flourish in the courts of our God.
They still bear fruit in old age; they are ever full of sap
and green, to declare that the L ORD is upright; he is
my rock, and there is no unrighteousness in him.*

PSALM 92:12–15 ESV

Dear Father,

Today, I want to claim this promise for my life. Because
I belong to You, I fall under the category of "righteous." This
verse states that the righteous will flourish. This means to be
in a vigorous state or to thrive. Please take the circumstances
that are causing me to worry and turn them around so I'll
thrive and so all my loved ones will thrive. I know You don't
always act instantly. I'll be patient, knowing and trusting that
You're working all things together for my good. Thank You
for Your promises, Father.

What do you picture when you think of yourself flourishing?

Springs in the Desert

*He turns a desert into pools of water, a parched
land into springs of water. And there he lets the
hungry dwell, and they establish a city to live in;
they sow fields and plant vineyards and get a
fruitful yield. By his blessing they multiply greatly,
and he does not let their livestock diminish.*

PSALM 107:35–38 ESV

Dear Father,

Right now I feel like I'm in a desert. I feel parched and hungry and needy. But You, Lord, are loving and kind and generous, and I know You will turn this desert of mine into a clear, spring-fed pond. You'll fill my hunger and calm my fears. In spite of what I feel right now, I know You have good things in store for me. Have mercy on me, Father. I'm hurting and scared. Please reach down and bless me right here, right now. My hope is in You alone.

*What part of your life feels parched and desert-like
right now? Picture it saturated with God's blessings.*

Every Moment

From the rising of the sun to its setting,
the name of the LORD is to be praised!
PSALM 113:3 ESV

Dear Father,

Praising You takes the focus off of myself and my problems and places it where it belongs. Praise is a lifestyle choice, and too often I make the wrong choice. Instead of praise, I choose worry and fear and anxiety and doubt. It's not a conscious choice, but I know when I choose to praise You and thank You for all the good things You've done, my fear dissipates. When I wake up in the morning, remind me to praise You. When I can't sleep at night, remind me of all the things I should be thankful for. Every moment of every day, I want to focus my thoughts on Your goodness, Your grace, and Your love.

What do you normally think about when you first wake up? Place a reminder by your bed to spend some time, first thing in the morning, praising God.

Call on Him

I love the LORD, because he has heard my voice and my pleas for mercy. Because he inclined his ear to me, therefore I will call on him as long as I live.

PSALM 116:1–2 ESV

Dear Father,

I do love You. I love You with all that is in me. I know You don't get angry at me when I worry about things. Instead, You invite me to share my thoughts, my fears, and my anxieties with You. You listen to every word, and You encourage me with reminders of Your love. I know my cries don't stop at the ceiling, but they reach Your ears the moment they escape. I call on You right now. You know my thoughts. You know every worry, every concern. Thank You for listening. Thank You for sending Your Holy Spirit as a comforter. And thank You for never getting tired of my pleas for mercy.

Do you call on God every single day? He wants you to.

Distressed

Out of my distress I called on the LORD; the
LORD answered me and set me free. The LORD
is on my side; I will not fear. What can man do
to me? The LORD is on my side as my helper;
I shall look in triumph on those who hate me.
PSALM 118:5-7 ESV

Dear Father,

    I could have written this psalm. Right now I'm in distress over so many things. Here, in the middle of my mess, I call to You. I know You are on my side, always working for my good. I know with You in my corner, I have nothing to fear. . .and yet I'm afraid. So here I am, talking to You, knowing You hear me. This simple act of prayer puts me in a better state of mind. Thank You for always being there for me. I love You, I trust You, and I know You have good things in store for my life.

What distresses you right now? Talk to God about it.

My Only Hope

*With my whole heart I cry; answer me, O LORD!
I will keep your statutes. I call to you; save me,
that I may observe your testimonies. I rise before
dawn and cry for help; I hope in your words.*

PSALM 119:145–147 ESV

Dear Father,

Sometimes it feels like You're not listening. I pray and pray. I cry to You with my whole heart. Please show Yourself, Lord. You are my only hope. You are the only one who can help me. I know You love me, Father. Please rescue me from this situation. You know every need and every detail, and I beg You to intervene. Give me patience as I wait for You to act. I know that even when it feels like You're ignoring me, You're not. You're always working on my behalf. I trust You, and in You I place all my hope.

*Do you truly believe God is working
on your behalf? He is. Trust Him.*

Toxic People

Too long have I had my dwelling among
those who hate peace. I am for peace,
but when I speak, they are for war!
PSALM 120:6–7 ESV

Dear Father,

Much of my worry, stress, and anxiety comes from within me. But I think part of it comes from being around toxic people. It's hard to break away from the negative people in my life. Some of them are permanent fixtures, and I don't know how to avoid them. Give me wisdom for how to act when I must be around them and how to stay away from them whenever possible. Help me pray for them instead of becoming like them. Whenever a conversation or climate turns hateful or negative, show me ways to turn things around in a way that honors You. I know by avoiding toxic people and situations, I'll alleviate much of the stress in my life.

Can you think of people or situations that increase your
anxiety? Talk to God about how to change your reaction.

In His Shadow

*The LORD is your keeper; the LORD is your shade
on your right hand. The sun shall not strike you
by day, nor the moon by night. The LORD will
keep you from all evil; he will keep your life.*

PSALM 121:5–7 ESV

Dear Father,

Shade is caused by something blocking the light. In order for a shadow to be present, something has to come between. I stand in Your shadow, don't I? You stand over me, blocking me from evil and protecting me from harm. I know I live in a fallen, broken world, and sometimes bad things will happen. But I also know You walk each step with me, sheltering me from the very worst of things. . .things I might not even be aware of. Thank You for keeping me in Your shadow. May I never leave the safety of Your presence.

*What do you need God to shade you
from? Talk to Him about it now.*

Quiet My Soul

O LORD, my heart is not lifted up; my eyes are not raised too high; I do not occupy myself with things too great and too marvelous for me. But I have calmed and quieted my soul, like a weaned child with its mother; like a weaned child is my soul within me.

PSALM 131:1–2 ESV

Dear Father,

David wrote this psalm. He was not worrying or occupying his thoughts with things that weren't his concern. Instead, he was calm, waiting, knowing that in the proper time, You would act. A child who isn't weaned cries the moment hunger hits. But the weaned child has learned to trust and waits calmly, knowing food will come. Thank You for David's wisdom in this scripture. Teach me to wait peacefully, calmly, knowing that in the proper time, You will act in love.

Do you concern yourself with things that aren't yours to manage? Take some deep breaths, calm yourself, and wait on God to act.

Live in Unity

Behold, how good and pleasant it is when brothers dwell in unity! It is like the precious oil on the head, running down on the beard, on the beard of Aaron, running down on the collar of his robes!

<small>PSALM 133:1–2 ESV</small>

Dear Father,

When oil was poured out on Your anointed one, it was a sign of Your approval. When the oil was abundant, it symbolized Your pleasure in that anointing. In the same way, You are pleased when your children get along well together. It makes You happy when we show love and kindness to each other. Father, there are some really difficult people in my life. Help me to live in unity with them as much as possible. Show me how to keep the peace without compromising my convictions. Most of all, make me a beacon of Your light, drawing them to You.

With whom do you have trouble getting along? Ask God to show you the best way to live in peace with everyone.

Like John

Now John wore a garment of camel's hair and a leather belt around his waist, and his food was locusts and wild honey. Then Jerusalem and all Judea and all the region about the Jordan were going out to him, and they were baptized by him in the river Jordan, confessing their sins.

MATTHEW 3:4-6 ESV

Dear Father,

John didn't worry about wealth, what he wore, or even what he ate. He didn't care what others thought of him. His only concern was what You thought. He wore rags and ate bugs, but he had a tremendous impact on Your kingdom. I'll bet he's wearing some fancy robes now and eating a king's feast! Even though he was considered poor, You cared so tenderly for his needs. Honey is considered a delicacy, after all. Thank You for caring tenderly for my needs as well. Help me follow John's example as I live for You alone.

Have you worried about earthly things instead of focusing on God's plan for your life?

God's Word

And after fasting forty days and forty nights, he was hungry. And the tempter came and said to him, "If you are the Son of God, command these stones to become loaves of bread." But he answered, "It is written, 'Man shall not live by bread alone, but by every word that comes from the mouth of God.'"

MATTHEW 4:2–4 ESV

Dear Father,

I know I can overcome temptation by filling my mind with Your Word. The more of the Word of God I know, the easier it is to recall scripture at times when I'm tempted. One of my weakest areas is the temptation to worry and not trust You. Satan tempted Jesus with bread when He was hungry, and he tempts me with worry when I'm stressed, anxious, and weak. Help me as I discipline myself to spend time in Your Word. Bring appropriate scriptures to my mind when I'm tempted to worry.

How much time do you spend reading God's Word? Make a plan today to read it regularly.

Getting Credit

"Thus, when you give to the needy, sound no trumpet before you, as the hypocrites do in the synagogues and in the streets, that they may be praised by others. Truly, I say to you, they have received their reward. But when you give to the needy, do not let your left hand know what your right hand is doing, so that your giving may be in secret. And your Father who sees in secret will reward you."

MATTHEW 6:2-4 ESV

Dear Father,

Too often, I worry about what others think of me. I want them to be impressed, so I do things in order to get credit. But my only concern should be what You think of me. Forgive me for wanting the spotlight. True humility does good things in private, without needing credit. Give me a humble nature. Help me honor You without worrying about what others think.

When is the last time you did something good without getting credit? How did it make you feel?

Trying to Impress

> *"And when you pray, do not heap up empty phrases as the Gentiles do, for they think that they will be heard for their many words. Do not be like them, for your Father knows what you need before you ask him."*
> MATTHEW 6:7-8 ESV

Dear Father,

Sometimes I want to impress others so they'll think well of me. I want them to think I'm good and kind and righteous and holy. I do good things, hoping for their approval. Forgive me for doing the right things with the wrong motives. Change my heart. Make me humble, because I know humility pleases You. Help me stop worrying about what others think and focus on honoring You with my thoughts, words, and actions. I want to be just like Jesus.

Do you care more about what others think or what God thinks? Do you need to shift your motives at all?

Forgiveness

"For if you forgive others their trespasses, your heavenly Father will also forgive you, but if you do not forgive others their trespasses, neither will your Father forgive your trespasses."

MATTHEW 6:14–15 ESV

Dear Father,

Forgiveness is a hard thing. It's an almost physical act, as I have to force myself not to hold things against others. Memories of hurtful deeds come up again and again, forcing me to forgive the same thing countless times. Help me to be diligent in the discipline of forgiveness. I want to forgive as many times as it takes, to truly remove all the anger I feel. I know holding on to unforgiveness causes me to feel anxiety. If You can forgive me for all the times I've hurt You, I know You can help me forgive others.

Whom do you need to forgive? Breathe in as you think of the hurt. Then ask God to help you breathe out forgiveness. Repeat this each time the memory enters your mind.

The Money Pit

"No one can serve two masters, for either he will hate the one and love the other, or he will be devoted to the one and despise the other. You cannot serve God and money."

MATTHEW 6:24 ESV

Dear Father,

I don't like to think of myself as a materialistic person. But I do worry about money a lot. I worry about bills, about retirement, about what will happen if someone in my family gets very ill. Yet You are my Father, and everything belongs to You. Why do I worry about these things when You've never let me down? I can see that by devoting so much of my time and attention to money, I'm allowing it to control me. Forgive me for giving more of my thoughts to money than to You. Each time I'm tempted to think about the almighty dollar, help me shift my thoughts to Your amazing generosity and love.

Do you worry about money? Ask God to provide.

Like the Birds

"Therefore I tell you, do not be anxious about your life, what you will eat or what you will drink, nor about your body, what you will put on. Is not life more than food, and the body more than clothing? Look at the birds of the air: they neither sow nor reap nor gather into barns, and yet your heavenly Father feeds them. Are you not of more value than they?"

MATTHEW 6:25-26 ESV

Dear Father,

All I need to do is look at nature, at Your tender care of all creation, to see Your kindness and generosity. The cardinal, in his majestic red coat, stands so tall and proud. Even the sparrow, in his humble brown, looks fat and happy, without a care in the world. They don't worry about material things. They know You will provide. Teach me to be carefree like the birds, trusting You completely for all I need.

*What physical thing do you need?
Leave it with God and trust Him to provide.*

What to Wear

"And which of you by being anxious can add a single hour to his span of life? And why are you anxious about clothing? Consider the lilies of the field, how they grow: they neither toil nor spin, yet I tell you, even Solomon in all his glory was not arrayed like one of these. But if God so clothes the grass of the field, which today is alive and tomorrow is thrown into the oven, will he not much more clothe you, O you of little faith?"

MATTHEW 6:27–30 ESV

Dear Father,

I admit it. I'm vain. I do worry about what I wear. Sometimes it's a matter of money, and I worry about how I'll afford the proper clothes for myself and my children. But this scripture passage is right, Father. You beautifully array all of Your creation, and I'm part of that creation. I'm Your child, and I know You'll provide everything I need.

What is your favorite outfit?
How did God provide it for you?

Trust Issues

"Do not worry then, saying, 'What are we to eat?' or 'What are we to drink?' or 'What are we to wear for clothing?' For the Gentiles eagerly seek all these things; for your heavenly Father knows that you need all these things. But seek first His kingdom and His righteousness, and all these things will be provided to you."

MATTHEW 6:31-33 NASB

Dear Father,

Anxiety reveals a lack of trust in Your goodness. Is there something in my past that causes me to struggle with trust? Though I can't untangle the web of thoughts and circumstances that bring me to this current place, You can. Heal me of my lack of trust, and help me to seek only You. Whenever worry plagues me, give me the strength to push it aside and focus on Your goodness.

Why do you think you struggle to trust God? Ask Him to heal you of the false belief system that causes you so much fear.

Wise Planning

*"So do not worry about tomorrow;
for tomorrow will worry about itself.
Each day has enough trouble of its own."*

MATTHEW 6:34 NASB

Dear Father,

Thank You for meeting all my needs so brilliantly and with such extravagance. Forgive me for focusing on the "what ifs" of my life when I need to focus on only You. I know it's wise to plan for the future, but wise planning does not mean useless worrying. Show me how to act wisely for my future without stressing or worrying over what might go wrong. Guide my actions and my thought processes. Make me shrewd but not anxious, smart but not worrisome. Right here, right now, I give it all to You. I trust You completely with today and every day to come.

*What can you do to wisely plan for your future?
Can you act in wisdom and trust God with the outcome?*

Ask

"Ask, and it will be given to you; seek, and you will
find; knock, and it will be opened to you. For everyone
who asks receives, and the one who seeks finds,
and to the one who knocks it will be opened."

MATTHEW 7:7-8 NASB

Dear Father,

Time and again in Your Word, You remind us of Your
generosity. You'll never withhold anything that I need to live
out Your perfect plan for me. I know that doesn't mean You'll
give me anything I want. It means You'll give me everything
that's required to fulfill Your purpose for my life. If I need
food and clothing and shelter, You'll provide it. If I need a
job, when I come to You in total and complete trust, You'll
provide that too. Thank You for Your generous love for me.
Most of all, thank You for Your gift of salvation. Really, that's
all I need.

*Do you feel God has withheld
something from You? Ask Him why.*

Through the Storm

And he said to them, "Why are you afraid,
O you of little faith?" Then he rose and rebuked
the winds and the sea, and there was a great calm.
And the men marveled, saying, "What sort of man
is this, that even winds and sea obey him?"
MATTHEW 8:26-27 ESV

Dear Father,

Why do I worry about anything? You control all, and Your care for me is intimate and complete. You love me, and You won't allow anything to consume or destroy me. Any difficulties I face are there to make me stronger. Like a wise coach, You encourage me through the struggle so I can build muscle and stamina, so I can feel proud and accomplished in the person I am in You and through You. When I think the storms will overtake me, I can call on You. You will either give me the strength to continue or cause the storm to abate. I trust You completely.

What storm do you face now?

Your Faith

When he had gone indoors, the blind men came to him, and he asked them, "Do you believe that I am able to do this?" "Yes, Lord," they replied. Then he touched their eyes and said, "According to your faith let it be done to you"; and their sight was restored.

MATTHEW 9:28–30 NIV

Dear Father,

If everything were done to me according to my faith, where would I be? Would I be stranded, alone, and destitute? That's how I act sometimes. My attitude reflects that I don't trust You very much. Thank You for not doing to me according to my faith. Instead, You show mercy and grace in spite of my weak trust in You. From here forward, let my actions reflect a strong faith in Your goodness, power, and love. That way, when You act according to my faith, I will see amazing things!

If God were to act according to the level of faith you exhibit, what would that look like? Ask God to help you adjust your attitude.

Words Matter

"You brood of vipers, how can you who are evil say anything good? For the mouth speaks what the heart is full of. A good man brings good things out of the good stored up in him, and an evil man brings evil things out of the evil stored up in him. But I tell you that everyone will have to give account on the day of judgment for every empty word they have spoken. For by your words you will be acquitted, and by your words you will be condemned."

MATTHEW 12:34–37 NIV

Dear Father,

If I stood before You today and You were to judge me based on my words, how would I measure up? So many of the things I say don't reflect the kind of faith I need to have. Instead, they exhibit worry, concern, and a lack of trust. Help me speak (and think) only faith in Your overwhelming power, goodness, and love.

*How can you adjust your speech
to reflect faith instead of worry?*

Sacrifice

"The kingdom of heaven is like treasure hidden in a field. When a man found it, he hid it again, and then in his joy went and sold all he had and bought that field."

MATTHEW 13:44 NIV

Dear Father,

This man sold all he had to buy a field because he knew the value of that field was worth giving up everything for. In the end, he gained far more than he lost. The same is true for my relationship with You. What if, instead of worrying about things, I just gave it all up to You? What if I stopped being concerned about myself and only focused on what pleases You? It would be a sacrifice, for sure. But in the end, I know I'll gain far more than I lose. Today, I want to give up all my worries and cares in exchange for unbridled, all-consuming faith.

How is giving up your worries a sacrifice? Is it worth the cost?

He Knows

He sent word and had John beheaded in the prison. And his head was brought on a platter and given to the girl, and she brought it to her mother. John's disciples came and took away the body and buried it; and they went and reported to Jesus. Now when Jesus heard about John, He withdrew from there in a boat to a secluded place by Himself; and when the people heard about this, they followed Him on foot from the cities.

MATTHEW 14:10–13 NASB

Dear Father,

How brokenhearted Jesus must have been to learn of such a brutal death for his beloved cousin. John spent his entire adult life telling others about Jesus, and now his life was over. Even though John fully lived out his purpose here, Jesus mourned his death. Jesus experienced sadness and heartbreak and the full gamut of human emotions. I know when I hurt or feel anxious or depressed, You understand. You've been there.

*What emotions do you feel right now?
Jesus knows. He understands. And He loves you.*

Even Better

*Now to him who is able to do far more abundantly than
all that we ask or think, according to the power at work
within us, to him be glory in the church and in Christ Jesus
throughout all generations, forever and ever. Amen.*
EPHESIANS 3:20–21 ESV

Dear Father,

I don't know why it's so hard for me to get it through my
head: You love me, You are generous and kind, and You are
able to do far more than anything I can think up. Worry is just
Satan's way of distracting me from that truth. You'd think I'd
learn, but for some reason, I keep listening to his lies. It's silly
for me to worry when I know Your solution to any problem
is far more amazing than the best scenario I can think of. I
praise You for Your goodness, Your power, and Your love.

*What's the best solution to your current problem
that you can imagine? God's solution is even better.*

Kingdom Keys

*"I will give you the keys of the kingdom of
heaven, and whatever you bind on earth shall
be bound in heaven, and whatever you loose
on earth shall be loosed in heaven."*

MATTHEW 16:19 ESV

Dear Father,

When you give someone the keys to something, you're giving them ownership. If they have the keys, they have power and control over it. When I believe. . .when I have faith. . .You give me the keys to Your kingdom and all that is in it. When I have faith in You, Your power supports me. When I have faith in You, Your authority lifts my status and allows me to have more control over any situation. Worry and fear give me a victim's status, but faith gives me a sense of dominance over my problems because I know Your strength belongs to me.

*In what situation have you felt powerless? Reframe
that situation in your mind, and picture yourself in
authority over that problem with God's full support.*

Mountain Mover

*Then the disciples came to Jesus privately and said,
"Why could we not cast it out?" He said to them,
"Because of your little faith. For truly, I say to you, if
you have faith like a grain of mustard seed, you will
say to this mountain, 'Move from here to there,' and
it will move, and nothing will be impossible for you."*
MATTHEW 17:19–21 ESV

Dear Father,

So many things in my life seem like impossible mountains.
I look at my problems and see something bigger than I am,
something that can't be moved, and I feel defeated. I need
to stop focusing on the size of the mountain and focus on
the size of my God. Any problem is nothing but a tiny anthill
from Your point of view. I may not be able to conquer my
difficulties, but You can. I put it all in Your hands. I can't wait
to see what You do.

*What mountain do you believe God will
move for you? Have faith that He can.*

Party Time

"Again I say to you, if two of you agree on earth about anything they ask, it will be done for them by my Father in heaven. For where two or three are gathered in my name, there am I among them."

MATTHEW 18:19-20 ESV

Dear Father,

You must be an extrovert! You like it when we get together and have prayer and praise parties. Forgive me for trying to carry my burdens alone. It takes humility to ask for prayer for myself. I don't want to share my worries and weaknesses with others. But when two or three people ask for the same thing, You show up! Give me a few trustworthy people that I can share my requests with. Help me to join them in praying for their problems as well. I look forward to seeing what happens when You come to the party.

What friends or family members can you share your concerns with? Will you commit to pray for them as well?

That Kind of Faith

*And Jesus answered them, "Truly, I say to you, if
you have faith and do not doubt, you will not only
do what has been done to the fig tree, but even if
you say to this mountain, 'Be taken up and thrown
into the sea,' it will happen. And whatever you ask
in prayer, you will receive, if you have faith."*

MATTHEW 21:21–22 ESV

Dear Father,

Where does my faith end? Do I believe You'll do some things but not others? The disciples were amazed at what Jesus did to the fig tree. Jesus said, "You think that's impressive? You ain't seen nothin' yet!" I want my faith to be so large, it has no borders. I want to believe that any problem, any giant can be obliterated with just a word from You. I want my faith to be infinite and unending. Give me that kind of faith, Lord.

*What problem seems too big for God?
Can you stretch the borders of your faith?*

Your Will Be Done

And going a little farther he fell on his face and prayed, saying, "My Father, if it be possible, let this cup pass from me; nevertheless, not as I will, but as you will."

MATTHEW 26:39 ESV

Dear Father,

Jesus was afraid. He didn't want to endure the things He knew were coming. Jesus understands fear and anxiety because He felt those things too. Still, He said, "Your will be done." Father, right now I lay it all on the table. I'm worried and afraid. Like Jesus, I beg You to "let this cup pass from me." I don't want to endure the things I'm afraid will happen. Yet I know You love me, and even through the fire, You will uphold me. You'll give me strength to endure what I must in order for Your perfect will to be accomplished. Like Christ, I pray that Your will is done.

What "cup" do you want to pass from you?
Are you willing to pray, "Your will be done"?

Cast Out

*And he healed many who were sick with various
diseases, and cast out many demons. And he would not
permit the demons to speak, because they knew him.*

MARK 1:34 ESV

Dear Father,

I know Your power still heals the sick and casts out
demons. I ask, with faith, please heal the diseases plaguing
me, my family, and all those I love. Cast out demons that are
causing havoc in my life. I know I have nothing to be afraid
of as long as You are on my side. Give me the kind of faith
that looks trouble in the face and casts it out in Your name.
I know I carry Your power within me, but often I allow that
power to lie dormant as I cower in fear. Give me the faith of
David as he stood against Goliath. I trust Your power, Lord.

*What sickness or problem needs healing
or casting out? Speak now, in Jesus' name,
believing in God's goodness and power.*

Compassionate God

And a leper came to him, imploring him, and kneeling said to him, "If you will, you can make me clean." Moved with pity, he stretched out his hand and touched him and said to him, "I will; be clean." And immediately the leprosy left him, and he was made clean.

MARK 1:40-42 ESV

Dear Father,

At this time in Jesus' ministry, He was a busy man. He traveled from town to town, preaching to crowds and sharing about Your great love. Everywhere He went, crowds pressed in to see Him. Yet He wasn't too busy or too important to care for the needs of this one man, a leper, an outcast. It's comforting to know You have compassion and that You care about my problems. Like the leper, I ask You now: if You will, please fix my problems and take away my fears. You're the only one who can.

What problem do you need to bring to Jesus today? He cares deeply about all your concerns.

Standard of Grace

And the Pharisees were saying to him, "Look, why are they doing what is not lawful on the Sabbath?" . . . And he said to them, "The Sabbath was made for man, not man for the Sabbath. So the Son of Man is lord even of the Sabbath."

MARK 2:24, 27–28 ESV

Dear Father,

Legalism is such a nasty trap. It causes me to compare myself to others and to some high standard I'll never be able to reach. This comparison, this high standard, is the root cause of much of my anxiety. It forces me on a hamster wheel of good works and unreachable goals and leaves me feeling like a failure. But that's not Your way, is it, Father? You have grace and mercy and compassion. You look at my heart rather than my abilities or even my actions. When You look at me, I hope You see someone who loves You and wants to please You.

What impossible standard have you tried to live up to?

Calming the Storm

And he awoke and rebuked the wind and
said to the sea, "Peace! Be still!" And the
wind ceased, and there was a great calm.
MARK 4:39 ESV

Dear Father,

Right now, I feel like there's a great storm in my life. It feels dangerous and out of control, and I want it to end. Everything is turbulent, and I feel I'll be tossed overboard at any moment. I worry with every breath, and I cry myself to sleep at night—if I sleep at all. I need You to say, "Peace! Be still!" to the storms in my heart, Father. Even as I pray, I feel Your power taking control of the tsunami, calming the winds, bringing peace to my thoughts and emotions. Thank You for quieting the hurricane inside my heart.

What hurricane is blowing inside your heart right
now? Listen closely for God to say, "Peace! Be still!"

A Good Trade

*Be anxious for nothing, but in everything by prayer
and supplication, with thanksgiving, let your
requests be made known to God; and the peace
of God, which surpasses all understanding, will
guard your hearts and minds through Christ Jesus.*

PHILIPPIANS 4:6-7 NKJV

Dear Father,

Be anxious for nothing. Really? I feel like I'm anxious for everything. Anxiety gets in my skin, in my bones. It acts like a filter, coloring everything I view. Good thing You offer the solution to this problem. In everything, I should pray. In everything, I should give thanks. In everything, I should tell You what I want—the deepest desires of my heart—and You will give me peace. This doesn't say You'll give me everything I ask for. But You'll exchange my worries for peace. Thank You for Your tender love that trades my worst for Your best.

*How would your days be different if they
were filled with peace instead of worry?*

Fear Not

*"Fear not, for I am with you; be not dismayed, for I am
your God. I will strengthen you, yes, I will help you,
I will uphold you with My righteous right hand."*

ISAIAH 41:10 NKJV

Dear Father,

As I read these words, I can almost hear a parent speaking to a small, frightened child. *"Shush! Don't be afraid. I'm right here. I've got you. See? I'm holding on to you."* The difference is, any earthly parent is flawed. An earthly parent is limited in power and influence. If imperfect earthly parents will do all in their power to protect their cherished child, how much more will You, the Almighty God, do to protect me? You gave the ultimate sacrifice—Your Son. Why do I question Your motives or Your desire to take care of every need in my life? Thank You for holding on to me, Father.

*Can you picture God holding you right now?
He loves you, and He will never let you go.*

Humility

*Therefore humble yourselves under the mighty hand
of God, that He may exalt you in due time, casting
all your care upon Him, for He cares for you.*

1 PETER 5:6–7 NKJV

Dear Father,

I love it when You give recipes. This passage provides a recipe for success. If I humble myself before You, You will exalt me in Your time. Much of my worry stems from wanting to exalt myself instead of waiting on You. I want that job, that promotion, that success—either for myself or for those I love. Worry stems from focusing on myself and my circumstances instead of focusing on You. Teach me what humility looks like. I know I can start by casting all my worries on You, leaving them in Your capable hands, and not thinking about them anymore. Thank You for Your tender, loving care over all my circumstances.

How can humility help alleviate your anxiety?

Joy in the Midst

*In the multitude of my anxieties within
me, your comforts delight my soul.*
PSALM 94:19 NKJV

Dear Father,

I'm so glad the psalmist wrote that he had a multitude of anxieties. Though I'm not happy for anyone to feel the way I do, it does make me feel less alone in my worries. The writer shared that even in the midst of all his worries and cares, he found comfort. Even more than comfort, he found delight. Can I really find joy in the middle of my fears? I believe I can, but only through You. Only when I totally and completely submit myself to You can I experience that kind of gift. Today, Father, I am Yours. I leave all my worries in Your hands. Thank You for Your comfort, which delights my soul.

*Have you ever felt joy and delight in
the middle of, or in spite of, your worries?
Ask God to help you experience that today.*

Who's in Control?

"Let not your heart be troubled;
you believe in God, believe also in Me."
JOHN 14:1 NKJV

Dear Father,

"Let not your heart be troubled." That command indicates I have control over whether my heart is troubled. It suggests I can govern the worries and fears that plague me. I think that's a lot of my problem, Lord. Instead of controlling my thoughts, I let my thoughts control me. Anything that flits through my mind becomes the boss of me, dictating my mood and even my actions. My lack of control indicates a lack of faith in You. Forgive me, Father. I believe in You. I trust You. I have faith in You alone. Today and every day, when anxious thoughts enter my mind, give me the strength and discipline to send them packing.

What is your foremost concern right now? What
can you do to keep that concern from dictating
your thoughts and actions? God is waiting to take
them from you if you'll just hand them over.

Finding Peace

"Peace I leave with you, My peace I give to you;
not as the world gives do I give to you. Let not
your heart be troubled, neither let it be afraid."

JOHN 14:27 NKJV

Dear Father,

Peace is a wonderful gift, but it seems just out of reach. Each time I think I've grasped it, it slips through my fingers. Perhaps that's because I'm looking to the wrong source. I seek that calm through my job, my relationships, my health, or my money. According to this verse, Your peace is already mine. You've already given it. And You don't give money or health or even earthly relationships as the source of peace because those things are temporary. The peace You give is in You alone, and You will never leave, never change. That's why I don't need to be troubled or afraid. Your love, Your peace is a permanent fixture in my life. All I have to do is hold on to You.

Who or what is your source of peace?

A Good Word

Anxiety in the heart of man causes depression,
but a good word makes it glad.
PROVERBS 12:25 NKJV

Dear Father,

My anxiety does tend to plunge me into depression. It causes me to not be my best self, to avoid other people, and to focus my thoughts on the negative. The second part of this verse—a good word—can come from a number of sources. Sometimes I wait for others to encourage me, but that's hit or miss. But Your Word is a constant source of encouragement for me. I don't know why I don't spend more time reading it. When I'm feeling worried, anxious, and depressed, bring Your Word to mind. Your words always bring me peace, comfort, and joy. In the same way, help me to always speak "good words" to other people as I seek to uplift them the way You uplift me.

What "good word" is God sending to your mind right now?
He loves you, and that's always a good place to start.

Only You

For in much wisdom is much grief, and he who increases knowledge increases sorrow.
ECCLESIASTES 1:18 NKJV

Dear Father,

This verse, written by King Solomon, seems kind of depressing. But when I think about its context, I understand what he was saying. Solomon spent much of his life seeking earthly knowledge and the wisdom of man, but in the end, it was all folly. He had all the riches he could desire, but it didn't bring him peace. I can relate. So much of my life is spent striving after things that, in the end, don't satisfy. Whether it's earthly wisdom, education, money, relationships, or health, none of it brings me the results I long for. Only You, Father, only You can bring me peace and serenity and joy. Help me learn from Solomon's mistakes and stop seeking things that won't quench my inner thirst. I only want to seek You.

What have you thought would bring you peace only to find you were wrong? Jesus Christ will never let you down.

True Life

Then He said to His disciples, "Therefore I say to you, do not worry about your life, what you will eat; nor about the body, what you will put on. Life is more than food, and the body is more than clothing."

LUKE 12:22-23 NKJV

Dear Father,

These words seem so simple when I read them. Yet they're hard to put into practice. I worry about what I eat, what I wear, how I'll pay my bills, what people think of me, and so many other things. Yet life is more than food, which will only satisfy me for a few hours. Life is more than clothing, which will get ripped and stained and eventually destroyed. True life is found only through a relationship with You. My focus should be on the eternal, not on the temporary. Help me shift my thinking to my relationship with You and trust You to take care of the rest.

What do you worry about most?
Can you trust God to take care of it?

Abundant Love

And God is able to make all grace abound toward you,
that you, always having all sufficiency in all things,
may have an abundance for every good work.
2 CORINTHIANS 9:8 NKJV

Dear Father,

Abundance. One dictionary defines it as an extremely plentiful supply; overflowing fullness; affluence; wealth. This verse promises that You'll make sure I have an abundance of whatever I need for every good work You've planned for me. Sometimes I long for abundance for my own selfish needs. You didn't promise to supply that. But You, in Your grace, will provide an overflowing amount of the things I need to help others, to be kind and generous, to work hard, to encourage the people around me. You'll supply everything I need to love like You love. Thank You for loving me abundantly so I can love others.

How has God loved you abundantly?
How can you show that abundant love to others?

Temporary or Eternal?

Therefore remove sorrow from your heart, and put away evil from your flesh, for childhood and youth are vanity.
ECCLESIASTES 11:10 NKJV

Dear Father,

This passage is all about focus. Solomon encourages young people to push aside the follies of this world, because those things that provide pleasure right here, right now, are only temporary. He even calls lustful things "sorrow," because he knows seeking after temporary pleasures will bring sorrow in the end. When I worry about things, in a way, I'm seeking temporary pleasure. Whatever I worry about, if the problem is fixed, I'll have a short-lived relief until another issue comes along for me to worry about. Help me stop wasting my time on those issues that won't matter in ten, twenty, or one hundred years. I want to focus on the permanent joy and peace that come from seeking You.

What are you most worried about? Does it have eternal significance, or is it only temporary?

What to Say

"But when they arrest you and deliver you up, do not worry beforehand, or premeditate what you will speak. But whatever is given you in that hour, speak that; for it is not you who speak, but the Holy Spirit."

MARK 13:11 NKJV

Dear Father,

I've never had to worry that I'd be thrown in jail or lose my life because of my faith. But I have been in positions where I worried I'd say or do the wrong thing and be judged harshly for it. In those moments, quiet my spirit, and help me listen to You. Let it be Your words that come out of my mouth, so others will know You are God. And please be with the people around the world who are in more dire circumstances for their faith. Give them peace, and give them the right words to say.

What conversation are you worried about?
God will provide the words if you trust
Him and follow His prompting.

Seed Among Thorns

*"Now he who received seed among the thorns
is he who hears the word, and the cares of this
world and the deceitfulness of riches choke
the word, and he becomes unfruitful."*

MATTHEW 13:22 NKJV

Dear Father,

I don't want to be like the person in this parable. I've heard Your Word. I've been shown Your way. But the things I worry about are like a thick veil over my eyes. They blind me to Your truth. They push me to forget what I know about You and cause me to lose my faith. I don't want to be a seed among thorns, Father. I want to be planted in the rich, fertile soil of Your truth. Worry and fear are not from You. When my focus strays to my worries, pull my gaze back to You. I love You, and I know You are more than able to take care of all my needs.

*How have you been like a seed among thorns?
How can you find more fertile ground?*

Forevermore

---

*And I heard a loud voice from heaven saying, "Behold,
the tabernacle of God is with men, and He will dwell
with them, and they shall be His people. God Himself
will be with them and be their God. And God will wipe
away every tear from their eyes; there shall be no
more death, nor sorrow, nor crying. There shall be no
more pain, for the former things have passed away."*
REVELATION 21:3–4 NKJV

Dear Father,

Thank You for this reminder that the last chapter
hasn't played out yet. You've already written the story in
advance, but the plot is still happening. You wrote these
words so I wouldn't worry. In the end, everything will be
okay. Everything will be better than okay as you wipe every
tear, right every wrong, and pour out Your love and peace
and grace and mercy on Your children, forevermore.

*Can you picture that day when God will
heal all your pain and wipe all your tears?*

For Eternity

Then Job arose, tore his robe, and shaved his head;
and he fell to the ground and worshiped. And he said:
"Naked I came from my mother's womb, and naked
shall I return there. The LORD gave, and the LORD has
taken away; blessed be the name of the LORD."

JOB 1:20–21 NKJV

Dear Father,

Thank You for this reminder that my problems are only temporary. All my fears and doubts, my worries and anxieties will one day melt away in Your presence. Even now, You've sent me Your peace. It's mine for the taking; I only have to accept it as I focus on Your great love. This life will soon pass away, and none of the things that seem so important now will matter at all. I want to live a life that matters for eternity. Blessed is Your Name, O Lord!

What things seem important now
but won't matter in eternity?

I Shall See God

*"For I know that my Redeemer lives, and He shall stand
at last on the earth; and after my skin is destroyed,
this I know, that in my flesh I shall see God."*

JOB 19:25-26 NKJV

Dear Father,

Why do I spend so much time thinking about temporary things, when this verse carries such truth? I know You live, Father. You've existed from the beginning of time, and You will be King for all eternity. Your presence is as real—and far more eternal—than my most pressing problems, my most worrisome fears. I can say this with confidence: one day, I will stand before You. I'll see You in the flesh. I'll hug You, and You'll hug me, and we'll spend all eternity loving each other. That's what I want to think about from now on.

*How do you think you'll feel when you see God
in the flesh for the first time? Bask in His love
right now, for you're already in His presence.*

Setting My Heart

*Set your hearts on things above, where Christ is,
seated at the right hand of God. Set your minds
on things above, not on earthly things.*
COLOSSIANS 3:1-2 NIV

Dear Father,

All too often, I do the opposite of what this verse commands. I set my heart on earthly things, and I get stuck there. That's Satan's plan, isn't it? He places worries right in my line of vision, hoping I'll take the bait and get hooked. And so many times, I bite. When those earthly fears and anxieties enter my mind, help me avoid the trap by setting my thoughts on You alone. Instead of worrying, I'll think about Your goodness. I'll praise You. I'll thank You for all the wonderful things You've done. Instead of setting the hook, help me set my heart on You.

*What is Satan's most common bait in your life
to distract You from focusing on Christ?*

No Fear

Fear of man will prove to be a snare,
but whoever trusts in the LORD is kept safe.

PROVERBS 29:25 NIV

Dear Father,

When I worry about other people and what they can do to me, when I'm afraid of what others may think of me, that shows a lack of trust in You. In Romans 8:31, I'm reminded that if You are for me, who can be against me? I don't know why I care so much about others when I should only care about what You think. I don't know why they make me so anxious when I have You on my side. Today, right now, I trust in You alone. I will not fear; I'll only trust. I am Your child. You have promised never to leave me or forsake me. I know as long as I stay close to You, You will take care of me.

Is there a person in your life who causes you
anxiety? Trust God, and let Him handle it.

For What Is Right

But even if you should suffer for what is right, you are blessed. "Do not fear their threats; do not be frightened."
1 PETER 3:14 NIV

Dear Father,

I've often suffered for my own poor choices. That's no fun, but I recognize my role in those trials. But sometimes I do my best to please You, to honor You, to live for You, and I suffer because of it. When that happens, it can feel like You've forsaken me, though You promised You wouldn't. It's hard to equate suffering with blessing, but I guess that's where faith comes in—faith in Your goodness. And faith in knowing You haven't finished my story yet. I know that despite my current hardships, my final chapter will be filled with blessings beyond measure. Give me courage through the fire, Lord. I trust You.

Have you ever suffered for doing what is right?
God knows. He sees. And He will bless you for it.

God Is for Us

If God is for us, who can be against us? He who did not spare his own Son, but gave him up for us all—how will he not also, along with him, graciously give us all things?

ROMANS 8:31-32 NIV

Dear Father,

This tells the whole story, doesn't it? You love me more than my mind can comprehend. It's a passionate love, a fierce love. You gave Your own beloved Son, Jesus. You traded His life for mine. He was the only One who could suffer death and conquer it in the end, so You sent Him to stand in my place. If You did that, how can I doubt Your love and care for me? How can I worry about trivial, temporary things, when You've already poured out Your bountiful, sacrificial love? My cares are minor in comparison. I know You're more than able to handle every trial I face. Thank You for that kind of love.

What fears dominate your thoughts?
Do you believe God can handle them?

Made for Power

For the Spirit God gave us does not make us timid,
but gives us power, love and self-discipline.
2 TIMOTHY 1:7 NIV

Dear Father,

You didn't make me timid or fearful. You didn't create me to be dominated by worries and anxiety. You created me to be powerful, loving, strong, and self-disciplined. If these worries aren't from You, they must be from the enemy. He wants me to live a defeated, fear-filled life, so he plagues me with thoughts that keep me from being my best self. I've been ruled by worry for so long, I don't know what it feels like to not be afraid. Teach me, Father. Show me what it means to be powerful and in control of my thoughts. Teach me to love You and others with a fierce, unmatchable love. I want to be strong, just as You made me to be.

Do you consider yourself a strong person?
Picture yourself wearing God's power everywhere you go.

Confidence

*"But blessed is the one who trusts in
the LORD, whose confidence is in him."*

JEREMIAH 17:7 NIV

Dear Father,

When I worry, I don't feel blessed. I guess that's because when I worry, I'm not blessable. I can't always choose the thoughts that enter my mind, but I can choose the thoughts I dwell on. From now on, instead of pausing on worry, fear, and anxiety, I will force those thoughts to the side and focus instead on Your goodness and power. I will set my mind on Your faithfulness, and I'll trust in Your love for me. To the best of my ability, I won't concern myself with anything but pleasing You. I know You will take care of me, and You'll handle my concerns in a far better way than I can imagine. You have my full confidence. Thank You for the freedom that comes with that kind of trust.

*Do your thoughts dwell on your fears? Force those
thoughts aside, and focus on God's great love for you.*